W9-AEQ-453

"Life's too short to wear boring shoes."

"A Flueflock of a Thousand Angels," an installation of water jet–cut, raw silver aluminum forms, created by Nathan Wiens's Chapel Arts in 2017, wings its way across the ceiling of the Victoria, BC store.
FACING The Chicago store

Signage at the Toronto Queen Street store
FACING The Brooklyn store

Toronto Distillery District store
FACING Signage at the Denver store

Abbot Kinney Boulevard in LA
FACING Being neighbourly in
San Francisco's Haight-Ashbury

John Fluevog with his first wife, Kecia Nyman, in the original Gastown store
FACING Good thoughts at the Denver store

KNOW
YOU'RE
WEIRD!

FLUEVOG.COM

Mural by Jef Martinez and
message by John at the
Manhattan store.
ACME Tools of the Trade
at the Toronto Distillery
District location.

For all the customers, weird, wonderful and everything in between,
who have supported me in keeping Vogville alive for fifty years.

UNIQUE SOLES FOR UNIQUE SOULS

50 years of unique soles for unique souls

FLUEVOG

JOHN FLUEVOG

St. John the Baptist Parish Library
2920 New Hwy. 51
LaPlace, LA 70068

TANGLE OF CONTENTS

(We don't always do things in order.)

INTRODUCTION

A FLUEVOG SHOE isn't just any shoe. It's not just something to get you from point A to point B. A Fluevog shoe makes a statement. It says, "I'm happy to make my own path, to dance to my own tune, to walk my way and no one else's." Sometimes, it just says, "I'm happy."

A Fluevog shoe is a well-made shoe. It's usually a pretty comfortable one, too. It stands out in a crowd with its unique shapes and vivid colours and handmade details. It looks at once retro and futuristic, orthopedic and sexy, practical and wildly whimsical. There is nothing else like it.

For starters, there's that name. "FLOO-vog." What does it mean? Where does it come from?

It's the moniker of one John Fluevog, who has been selling, making and designing shoes on the edge of the continent, in Vancouver, Canada, since 1970. Today he has twenty-seven stores in Canada, the United States, Amsterdam, and now Melbourne, Australia, as well as a thriving online retail business. His boutiques are some of the last independent stores left anywhere in the world where the owner is also the designer. His business and brand are truly unique.

There is a worldwide Fluevog subculture. Fluevogers recognize each other through their cute Minis and glam Munsters, their jaunty Derby Swirls and the toe bump on a Swordfish boot. As soon as they recognize a kindred spirit, the stories start. They reminisce about where they bought their first Vogs and commiserate over the unicorn that got away. They shop for pre-loved Vogs at the FlueMarket; they peruse the Flueblog and vote on VogPopuli; they look up styles of yore in the Flueseum, perhaps with the help of a Fluevogologist.

Funnily enough, the family name wasn't Fluevog to begin with. It was Nielsen. Could you imagine? Shoes by John Nielsen? Those would be pretty boring shoes, don't you think?

Turns out *Fluevog* works pretty well as a noun, an adjective and a verb. It's odd and slightly comical. It's just difficult enough to say that you'll never forget it, but not so tricky you'll give up trying. It conjures the idea of little animals: there's a little fluevog, how cute! And kids love that *F* thing. So do grownups, come to think of it.

> **"The first time I worked with John, I asked for wooden clog styles. John said, 'No problem.' He hand-carved them himself in his garage!"**
>
> ANNA SUI, FASHION DESIGNER

It's cute and it's fun, but don't be fooled: John Fluevog Shoes is also serious business.

John Fluevog started out selling shoes—really cool shoes—in the historic part of Vancouver known as Gastown. He was the first to bring Dr. Martens to Canada, maybe to North America. He was one of the first to start selling shoes online, too. He tapped into hippies and disco, punk and grunge and house.

> **"John and I started designing shoes the same year. We both wanted to change the world in our own ways. John designed shoes with a very strong point of view. I respected John for his courage, his consistency, his values, and always sticking to 'his last.'"**

ALDO BENSADOUN, FOUNDER, ALDO SHOES

But he had an untapped artistic bent of his own, a love of unusual shapes and lines and bold colours, and it was only a matter of time before he started designing his own shoes. You've seen them on Lady Miss Kier and Madonna, on Alice Cooper, Jack White and Lady Gaga. You might also have seen them on your lawyer, your doctor, your dentist, on the person who teaches your kids music and the barista who's making cappuccino art at the hip new joint in your neighbourhood.

Fluevogers are everywhere. They're just not everyone.

John Fluevog is an astute businessman, but not a conventional one. His journey to commercial success has not been easy or straightforward. He has loved and lost, hovered on the edge of bankruptcy more than once, and even skirted the law to keep things afloat. Angels have been there to help him when things have been particularly hard. He believes it's because his journey is not yet done, that he has more to say, more to do.

Speaking of saying things. Many of his shoes come with a message. The messages are the essence of John Fluevog. They are a little bit corny, a whole lot heartfelt, and a much-needed antidote to this most cynical of eras: "Stay sharp!" "To love or to hate, the choice is yours." "Share your cool…increase your daily hugs." "Reach for the extraordinary." "Don't delay, Fluevog today."

In conversation, John Fluevog unselfconsciously scatters words like *mystic*, *dreams*, *humanity*, *poems*, *childlike*, *colour*, *shape*, *love*, *community* and, above all, *faith* and *spirituality*. He is a romantic who adores his family and still gets starry-eyed when he remembers a woman who walked into his store nearly five decades ago. He wears his spirituality like a cozy cardigan, a comforting layer that kept him warm when the world was cold and now is just part of his everyday ensemble. He has made money by quietly giving it away, supporting people and causes that speak to his soul. His sole.

John Fluevog's world—call it the Fluniverse, or maybe Vogville—is unique. It has its own language. It has its own international day (May 15—John thinks you should celebrate with random acts of kindness). Its citizens come from all walks of life, but none hews to the ordinary. It is a world of happy colours, bold shapes and sensual lines. It is a world where nothing is too ridiculous to try, where comfort and wearability matter as much as how good something looks. Goodness matters in the Fluniverse, and kindness, and God, however you choose to define God.

John Fluevog began his journey fifty years ago when he and Peter Fox opened a shoe store in a historic Vancouver neighbourhood. And he's just getting started.

This is his story.

— Joanne Sasvari, lifestyle journalist

INTERNATIONAL FLUEVOG DAY
MAY 15, 2017
GASTOWN
65 WATER STREET VANCOUVER
NO YOU'RE WEIRD

Celebrating International
Fluevog Day across the
country

INTERNATIONAL FLUEVOG DAY
MAY 15, 2018
180 SAINT PAUL OUEST, MONTREAL

UNIQUE SOLES FOR UNIQUE SOULS

In the beginning there was John Fluevog, grandson of pioneers, exploring his Vancouver backyard and the great beyond. In the 1950s and '60s, he discovered his love of cars, fashion and music, and was ready to set foot on his great journey as a master shoe designer.

*Your Sole
will direct
your future*

1

BEFORE THE
BEGINNING

1948–1969

I KNOW WHAT PEOPLE SAY ABOUT MY SHOES: Creative. Original. Funky. Sassy. Groovy. Artistic. The funny thing is, I didn't have a clue that I was artistic until I was in my thirties. I didn't even really like artistic people. I thought they were kind of sketchy.

It turns out that I'm both practical and creative. That was quite a discovery for a kid who was dyslexic and bad in school, who almost didn't graduate and who never really knew what he wanted to be when he grew up. A lot of my life was me not thinking I was good at things, then finding out later that I actually was.

It's been fifty years since I've been selling and making shoes, and after all this time, I've just started to understand who I am. It's taken me this long to realize that my business has been my spiritual journey. Now I want to encourage and maybe inspire others who are setting foot on the same path.

So let's start at the beginning. No, let's start before the beginning.

I was born on May 15, 1948, to Ruth and Sigurd Fluevog, in the city of Vancouver, British Columbia, on the far-left coast of the North American continent. My sister Gail followed three years later and my brother Glen five years after that. We have an older sister, too, Karen, who was born in 1943.

We had a very free childhood. Even when I was little, I rode my bike everywhere. We lived at 6th and Fraser and one day, when I was eleven or so, I rode my bike all the way from home across what was then known as the Second Narrows Bridge, up that steep hill to North Vancouver and back again. Must have been twenty kilometres, maybe more. The bridge, which spans the Burrard Inlet, had just been finished, and it was crazy and dangerous and a little bit scary. But we just went off and did stuff like that back then.

My dad was an eccentric character, really smart, and a big personality, the kind of guy who was never embarrassed by a moniker like Sigurd Cornelius. It's royalty, right? That's the kind of man he was. He was a huge influence in my life—it took me a long time to get over being Sigurd's son, because that's what I was, Sigurd's son. I didn't have an identity of my own for a long, long time. Where Sigurd was often critical and demanding, Mom was loving and kind; she encouraged us, whatever we decided to do, as long as we were good and believed in God.

They were both devout Christians—in fact, my mother always said she married my dad because he was the only true Christian around. Their faith was a huge influence on me as a child and for a long time after that. Even now.

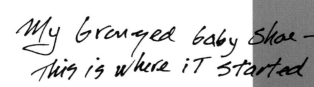

My Greenyed baby shoe— this is where it started

1948

John Fluevog is born to parents Sigurd and Ruth in Vancouver, BC. He has an older sister, Karen, and two younger siblings, Gail and Glen. To future generations, May 15 will become known as International Fluevog Day.

My parents grew up in rural Alberta farm country—Dad in Irma and Mom in Kinsella—but my grandparents were pioneers in the truest sense of the word. My father's parents came from Norway and homesteaded in South Dakota and Minnesota before heading up to Alberta. Their name was originally Nielsen, but there were so many other Nielsens in Minnesota, the mail kept getting mixed up. So my grandfather, Nikolai Tobias Mathias, changed it to Fluevog, which was inspired by the name of the tiny hamlet back in Norway where the family came from. There's also a little lake up in Alberta, near where my grandparents homesteaded, called Fluevog Lake. I never met my father's folks, though I wish I had. They died back in the 1930s when my dad was in his twenties; my dad always told me his mother, Gina, died first, and then his father died of heartache. My grandfather was tender-hearted, and I think I'm that way myself.

On my mother's side, they were Dutch and German with a bit of Irish thrown into the mix. When he was just eight years old, my grandfather, Ben Wachter, drove horses and mules along the Oregon Trail all the way up to Wilbur, Washington. He eventually became a farmer in Alberta and worked building the railways. He was truly a pioneer. My grandma, Clara, was a big, imposing woman who came from St. Louis, Missouri, and after she married Ben, she stayed home to look after the house and family. When we were kids, we'd go on lots of road trips to the farm. It had no running water or paved roads, but tons and tons of bugs. It was as natural as can be. In summer, it would get so hot when we were driving, we'd cook chuckwagon dinners on the manifold. At Christmas, it would be too cold to drive to church, so we'd go out with the horse and sleigh.

My grandparents were pioneers in the truest sense of the word.

My parents met skating one day back in Alberta. Sigurd was seven years older than Ruth, and both were ready to marry; in the end, they had fifty-four mostly happy years together. My mom was a good cook, generous host, talented seamstress and bit of a poet. My dad was a great mechanic and really smart, so smart that during the Second World War, he was sent

A (very) young John Fluevog discovers his love of cars in his dad's garage, where Sigurd sold cute Hillmans from England.

on the "65" Jag

My 1948 Austin I still drive it most days. If I can keep it going then maybe.....

So nice they named it twice!

to Bella Bella, a remote village in the rainforest along the British Columbia coast, to decode secret Japanese messages. My sister Karen was born up there. After the war, they moved to Vancouver, where my dad opened his own garage near the Kootenay Loop, at Hastings and Boundary. He loved anything that had wheels and sold these cute English cars called Hillmans. I've inherited his love of cars and all things mechanical.

In 1952, when I was just four years old, he opened a soft-serve ice cream place on Kingsway in Burnaby, British Columbia. It was called the Luxury Freeze Drive-In and it became a real scene. Everyone went to the Luxury Freeze. They'd go to socialize and, most of all, to show off their cars. There were lots of custom cars loaded with fashion statements like fancy grills and doodads and dingle balls. Cars were a real status symbol in the 1950s. You could be unpopular, but if you had a cool car you could get a pretty girl to drive around with you. My dad and I shared a love of cars, and by the time I was ten, I knew everything about every model that would pull into the drive-in. Now I realize that's where I kind of developed a feel for shapes and lines and the feelings they create.

I spent a lot of time hanging around the Luxury Freeze. My dad was basically my babysitter, and as I watched him work, I learned a lot from him, both what to do and what not to do. He did everything by himself. He never hired anybody. He considered it evil to spend the money when he could do it himself. Besides, he always thought he could do things better himself. It wasn't always true, of course, but he did teach me one of the most important lessons of my life: If you want to do something, you just start. There's nothing you can't do if you really want to.

The Luxury Freeze was where I kind of developed a feel for shapes and lines and the feelings they create.

The Luxury Freeze was super successful, not just as a business, but as a place where my dad could spread the gospel because, of course, he was still a good Christian. My parents were good-looking and could have been a real power couple, if they'd wanted to. Everyone knew my dad. Everyone knew Sig. He talked to everyone and, by the time I became a teenager, that

I'm still not good at spelling.

8 yrs old

My heart throb

me

Sigurd Fluevog closes his garage and opens the Luxury Freeze Drive-In. The soft-serve ice cream joint becomes the cool place in the city for people to hang out and show off their cars. John becomes fascinated with the stylish cars, fashion and music of the 1950s.

1952

was super embarrassing to me, especially when he talked about religion. It embarrassed me that my parents were religious. I didn't want to be religious. I wanted to fit in. And people who were religious were weird, right?

Our house was a non-stop train station, always full of teenagers and prayer meetings. And music! Dad played piano, and music was a big deal in our house. He'd make us sit around the piano at night and sing in three-part harmony. My two sisters were both good at the piano, too. I never learned how to play it. I was in choir, though. In fact, I was the leader of the junior choir. Crazy, huh?

Even though I wasn't very good in school, I did like band class, and my teacher took a shine to me. I played trumpet. I wasn't good at reading notes because of my dyslexia, but I was good at playing. I played my trumpet at events, weddings and church services. I'd wail away on it and people loved it. Who'd a thunk? I always say it's a good thing I wasn't good at playing the guitar because I would have been in a rock 'n' roll band and it would have all been downhill from there.

There was lots of music around the Luxury Freeze, too. Buddy Holly. The Everly Brothers. Little Richard. I remember hearing Elvis Presley sing "Don't step on my blue suede shoes" in 1956 and being really blown away by that. Maybe that's what drew me to shoes in the first place.

Then, in 1958, there was a fire at the Luxury Freeze. Even though my dad got plenty of insurance money to rebuild, the energy just went out of him. Two years later, he sold it, and my family moved out to the suburbs, to South Burnaby. At the same time, he went through something of a religious awakening. It was good, and not all that good.

Around 1961, my dad went to Bible school. And then things kind of went sideways for him. He got sick with rheumatoid arthritis and ended up on a disability pension for the rest of his life, which made him bitter, especially having railed his whole life against low-lifers on the government dole. Meanwhile, he was determined to become a minister and thought I should be one, too. It was the 1960s, though, and that wasn't going to happen.

Instead, right around then, in my teens, I decided I was going to be bad. I wasn't super bad. Mostly, I had this dual life of being Mr. Cool and Mr. Christian Kid. I wasn't good in school—I couldn't add two and two and get four. My grades weren't good. I raised a ruckus in class. I was the class clown. Disruptive. A tough kid. Sometimes I'd even pick on kids on the way home from school, but I wondered even then why I did it. Like I said before, a lot of my life was me not thinking I was good at things, then finding out later that I actually was. I didn't do sports.

Yes! I had a "60s" surfer haircut

Fire devastates the Luxury Freeze; his father rebuilds, but loses his passion for it.

Sigurd sells the Luxury Freeze and the family moves to South Burnaby.

Sigurd goes to Bible school; John decides to become a troublemaker.

In high school, John discovers that he's a terrible student, but a snappy dresser who was into cars and good at band. Later he realizes that he has a sort of dyslexia that makes classroom learning a challenge.

I was terrible at them anyway. I took things apart and customized them. Even when I was little, I'd change the shape of all my Dinky cars—I'd flatten them, shorten them, take off the doors, cut off the roofs, anything to make them different.

Back then, no one really knew about things like dyslexia. I never even heard about it until I was in my twenties, and now I think maybe that was a factor when I was a kid. That, or a kind of hyperactivity that should have been treated way back when. I still can't focus on anything for very long.

But I was Sig's kid, so I worked hard, even if it wasn't in class. All the way through high school I had a job. For a while I was stocking paper at Smith Davidson & Lecky, a paper wholesaler in Yaletown, when Yaletown was still a neighbourhood of warehouses and factories, and not cool restaurants and condos like it is now. And then I worked in a factory cutting newsprint on Granville Island, when it was an industrial area, before the public market opened.

I finished high school in 1968—barely. I failed Grade 12 once and took it again and I can't even remember if I graduated. I think I graduated from a general program, but I never had the grades to go to university. It was twelve years of misery, actually. I had no idea I had any talents, aside from chasing girls. And you can't make a living chasing girls.

For a while, I worked at a mill on the Fraser River. I thought I was a tough kid, but that job almost killed me. All day I'd feed logs to the men on the bandsaws, and they'd be yelling at me because I couldn't get them the wood fast enough. It was dangerous and it was cold and wet and I was sick all the time. I've never been a quitter, but I had to quit that job.

And then somehow I ended up in Hawaii, on this boat trip with kids from all over the world. It was amazing. Here I was, nineteen years old, from Vancouver, which back then was in the middle of nowhere, meeting kids from Europe and America. It opened my eyes and made me realize there was more to life, and a much bigger world out there than I'd imagined.

By the time September of 1969 rolled around, I was restless and hungry for something new. So when a flashy scientist from a California university came up to speak in Vancouver, I was ready to buy what he was selling. And what he was selling was a whole new way of looking at the world.

He was a seeker, a Christian, and I guess you'd call him a guru. It was the '60s, after all, and Vancouver was a magnet for the counterculture, for all the hippies and

Before and after: the Jag then, and now the Fluevos

Sigurd buys the Jaguar Mark X that John would later transform into "The Fluevog."

John finishes high school, eventually. He takes a life-changing trip to Hawaii, where he joins a boat full of kids from all over the world and discovers that the world is both bigger and more easily within reach than he'd thought.

dropouts and draft dodgers that ended up here on the edge of the continent. Anyway, he was speaking at Simon Fraser University and my friends suggested I go hear him. He was mesmerizing. His version of transcendental (and possibly drugged-up) Christian spirituality was so different from my parents' old-fashioned by-the-Bible Christianity, it seemed like it might be the answer to what I was looking for, at least for a while. He was cool, for an older guy, and he was surrounded by even cooler young people, drawing them to him like Christ and his disciples. I was at loose ends. So when he invited me down to his compound in California, of course I said yes.

I hopped into my Citroën ID (even then I had a cool car, though not really a cool car for a teenager) and headed down the highway to San José. I'm not sure now what I expected, but it wasn't what I found: a commune, all young men, living together in this lovely adobe house with big glass windows, sleeping together, dropping acid. When he made a move on me, I realized this wasn't my scene. I was a goofy kid, what did I know? I hardly knew what homosexuality was.

I needed to find a way to get out of the house, so I got a job washing dishes at a twenty-four-hour restaurant. I also looked up a girl I'd met in Hawaii, who lived nearby, and we started seeing each other. One night I was coming home from her place around one in the morning, driving along Arastradero Road, which is like the Kingsway of San Jose. As I crossed an intersection, something flashed right in front of my face. It looked like a wire wheel. I turned the car around and realized the intersection was actually a T-junction, with a parking lot on one side. I looked closer and there was an E-Type Jag on the roof of a house. A man and woman were in it, totally inebriated, not a scratch on them. She'd been driving through the parking lot and hit a log; she was going so fast, at least a hundred miles an hour, that they'd become airborne. That car was so close to me, if I'd been ten seconds, maybe five, ahead, I would have been dead. I think of that flash now as divine intervention.

It also made me realize it was time to go home. It was the end of 1969. The Summer of Love was long over, and so was my California adventure. So I got in my car and drove back to Vancouver, all the way in the rain, without windshield wipers. I got back just in time for Christmas, parked the car and the axle broke. It never moved again.

I was twenty-one years old and it was time to figure out what I was going to do with the rest of my life. But what, I wondered, was that going to be? JF

This could have been "THE END!"

John meets a Christian guru, who invites him down to his place in California. John hops in his Citroën ID and heads to San Jose, where he finds a house full of young men, expanding their minds. It turns out not to be his scene, and after a terrifying near-miss while driving, he returns home to Vancouver in time for Christmas and the next step on his journey.

1969

THE SHOES

*Step into the world of John Fluevog and discover
some of his most iconic footwear.*

In fifty years we have created more than three hundred shoe families and thousands of different shoe styles. That's a lot of funky footwear. Each year, I start a new sketchbook. I come up with the initial sketch, the feeling of the season. My ideas are like a clear, pure stream that trickles down a mountain and across the desert floor. Then the design team gathers that stream of ideas and makes them into shoes. I also write the messages— I call them "the thoughts of the season"— and put them on some of the shoes. It's these messages that are the essence of the brand.

PREVIOUS PAGE A display of shoes at the Ottawa store, just steps away from the centre of government, the House of Commons

FIVE KEY KICKS

1

Pilgrim

This super-pointy-toed, buckled T-strap loafer was the first shoe I designed for women, back in 1986. It was based on a Victorian design with cowboy boot influences. It's still one of our best sellers thirty-five years later, although it has updated features like the rubber sole plate and 1.25-inch leather-wrapped heel. Today it's part of the Truth family, which is full of straight-up winners like the Eileen, a zip-up ankle boot with ornate buckles. "Truth and integrity since 1970."

2

Munster

You know the Munster. It's the platform shoe with the sexy, oversized Louis XIV heel that was made famous first by Lady Miss Kier, who wore them on the cover of Deee-Lite's 1990 debut album, *World Clique*, then by Madonna who flaunted them in the 1991 movie *Truth or Dare*. It was the first shoe I made completely from scratch, from sketch to mould, back in 1988, and it became the symbol of the 1990s house/club underground DJ scene. Now known as the Mega Munster, the Original is best remembered in classic suede and special edition glitter, and has been joined by variations like the T-strap Elektra and Clique. "Groove is in the heart."

3

Swordfish

As dangerous as it is dashing, the Swordfish dates back to the late 1980s, a rebellious, pointed-toe shoe that's been reimagined with a distinctive toe bump. These are the rock star royalty of the Fluevog lineup, with descendants like the Imperial and Marquess lines. Comes in every style from dagger-sharp lace-up shoes to chukka and knee-high boots. Alice Cooper has rocked the Swordfish for decades, and Lady Gaga sported the Cubist Cupcake version, a smooth women's lace-up boot with buckle, in fall 2016. "Stay sharp!"

4

Mini

Small in name but huge in impact, the Mini was the shoe that turned everything around for Fluevog Shoes in the early 2000s. It's cute, but it's also tough and comfortable, the favourite choice of women who have to be on their feet all day and want to make a statement while they do it. The Mini and its clan can be identified by their sturdy medium-height hourglass heel and, as often as not, bright, whimsical colours and patterns. The Gorgeous, for instance, is a durable, round-toed Mary Jane, while the Babycake is an adorable buttoned boot named for our baker friend who makes the best cupcakes in Canada. "Go on, fall in love. We dare you!"

5

Angel

One thing we know for sure, Angels walk among us. The original Angel sole, designed around 1992, has begat many cherubs, all handcrafted, clean-lined and floating on all-natural latex soles that have been called the most comfortable on the planet. In fact, it's the sole that makes this shoe an Angel, because there are many different styles. There are Angels for men and Angels for women. City Angels and Urban Angels, Future Angels and Guardian Angels. The Little Wing is a moccasin-stitched boat shoe Angel. The Manhattan is an asymmetrical lace-up derby Angel. The 7th Heaven family is descended from the original Angels and adds rubber to the mix; it features offspring like the Michael, a classic brogued wing-tip derby, and the Supervog, a classic style with Super Swirl details on each side, a padded tongue and collar for comfort and a snug fit. "Angels resist alkali, water, acid, fatigue and Satan."

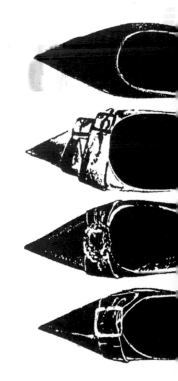

Lasts and firsts at the Brooklyn store,
including the Cubist Cupcake bootie
(*opposite page, far right*) and a snapshot
of a famous fan

Every shoe starts with a sketch, like these drawings that would join the Kitschy Kitschy Boom Boom, Bellevue, Fairway and Enneagram families.

At the Amsterdam store,
Enneagrams in all their
colourful glory

The Malvern, a 2016 Oxford with broguing, a Swordfish toe bump and shimmery leather

RADIO
Practical. Unassuming. Essential. The classic hits keep on coming from this handsome family. "Tune in, turn on, and Vog out!"

DELIVERANCE
A Western vibe, vintage inspired, with curved lines and a retro Rococo heel. "Share your cool… increase your daily hugs."

DRIVEN
Named for famous drives (Atlin, Coquihalla, Sea to Sky, Crowsnest, Muskoka, Algoma). Put pedal to the metal. "Driven to do it!"

CONQUER
Your ultimate girl power boots. Conquer your insecurities with their zigzag soles and studded wedge heels. "Pick your battles!"

WEAREVER
Magnificently evolved and at peace with it, these are not-so-classic buckled shoes that are both sexy and functional. "Wearever you go, give thanks."

POWER/POWER UP
The power of sleek, casual style. These are total game changers crafted from soft and nappa leathers. "You have the power to change the world."

KICKBACK
Laidback, sweet and spiffy, this is our take on the urban sneaker. "Reach for the extraordinary."

MODVOG
One part responsible, two parts reckless and three parts awesome, this family evokes styles of the '60s. "Don't gamble with your sole."

BIG PRESENCE
This family pays tribute to brave and daring women with bold and gallant designs. Think elegant Mary Janes and beautiful pumps. "Present yourself well."

FLIGHT
The cozy, casual but luxurious kicks you want to wear when you have a flight to catch. "When you fly Fluevog, you always fly first class."

LUXURY FREEZE
An homage to my father's frosty drive-in. Full of deep flavour and plenty of sweet details like custom embroidery and painted heels. "Cool on a hot date."

BALTHAZAR
Asymmetric and sculptural, yet comfortable. "Balthazar, a mystic traveller following a star bearing gifts from afar."

LIVING AND LIVING 2.0
My philosophy has always involved bringing attention to the many things that inspire me on a daily basis. Check out the Babette ankle boot (for men or women) with its faux laces and zip-up side. "Living to change the world."

ENNEAGRAM
Like the personality test, these shoes are designed to connect to your inner soul. With names like Investigator, Individualist, Optimist, Enthusiast and Peacemaker, they are cute and comforting all at once. "Be your true self."

Other favourite shoe families

SLACKER
Just because something comes together at the last minute doesn't mean it's not worthy of admiration. This family comprises the lace-up Tardy and Procrastinator, and the easy slip-on Nap with its no-non-sense crepe soles. "Let it go!"

HOPEFUL
Lower block heels that mix a polished dreamboat vibe with relaxed elegance. *"F is for all things that give hope."*

FUTURE ROUND TOE
Easy to wear, one step forward, two steps fashion forward in these comfy kicks. "Know the future, decide well today."

WONDERS
Curved lines, playful, elegant, classically inspired but completely original. "You are a natural wonder."

COSMOS
Classic and flattering from every angle, with a signature Cosmos heel. "Created in the cosmos, worn on Earth."

POSER
Posers are sweet and elegant, just like you on a first date. They're cute and sleek, made with love, an hourglass heel and a kick of power. "Yes, you are. You're super cute. I said so."

CHOICE
Who doesn't want choice in life? Wise yet frivolous, like the Adele, a low-heeled Mary Jane with specialty leather uppers and grosgrain ribbon lace. "To love or to hate, the choice is yours."

MISSION
A Mary Jane with an angel sculpted into its rubber heel, the Wendy is named for my dear friend Wendy, who died too soon, but completed her mission in life. "A real feat for your feet."

BELLEVUE
Named for grand dames like notable Texan gambler Lottie Deno and Ella Baker, an outspoken activist of the American civil rights movement. "Keep pushing west and beyond your imagination."

The 1970s were a decade of upheaval in Vancouver—and in John Fluevog's life. He'd finally started on his life journey in fabulous footwear, and along the way found love, and loss, and love again. He was ready to make history.

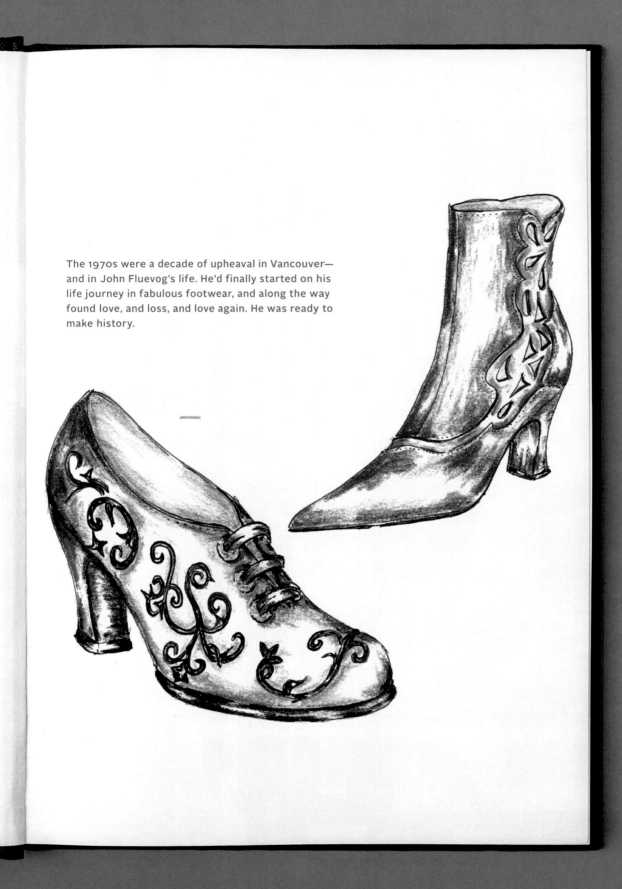

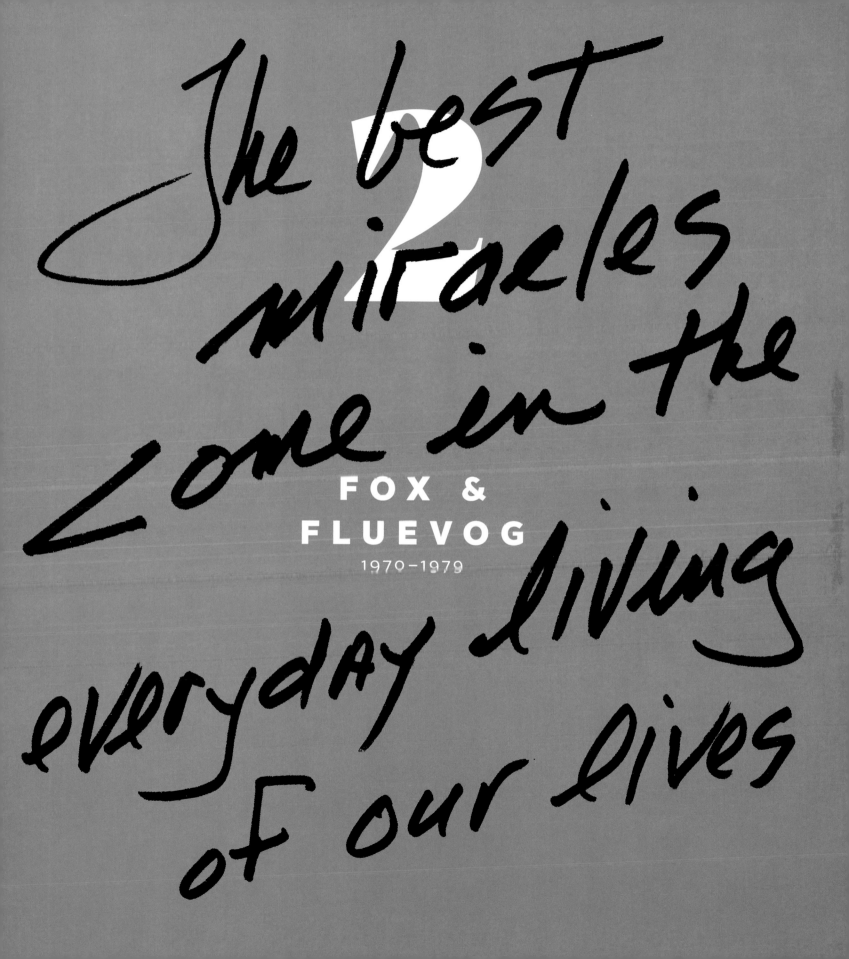

The best miracles come in the everyday living of our lives

2

FOX & FLUEVOG
1970–1979

WHEN I GOT HOME FOR CHRISTMAS OF 1969, I had no plan for the future or any idea of how I'd get one. It was grey and rainy and cold, the way Vancouver is in December, when one day I joined my parents at their church. It's a good thing I did, because that was the day I met Peter Fox. And that would change everything.

Peter was a friend of my parents, but more than that, he was the manager of Sheppard Shoes, the high-end men's shoe store where everyone who mattered in town would shop. He was born in London, and was very cool, with his English accent, granny glasses and bespoke suits. He was an artist, too. He'd studied sculpture at art school in London in the 1950s and worked at Harrods's shoe department, before coming to Vancouver. We got to talking and found that we shared a fascination with shape and line. As it turned out, he had the crazy idea of opening a menswear boutique—a cool one, not the same old tweedy stuff everyone else was selling, but not tie-dye and ponchos either—and he asked me, would I be interested in a job? Well, yes, of course I was.

They tell me now that I seemed so arrogant back then, but it was because I was insecure. I'd drive Peter to work in my two-seater sports car, a 1953 MG TD, which was a vintage car even back then, and I'd be dressed in these super flashy clothes, like this double-breasted suede jacket I used to love. It was the hippie era, but I wasn't a hippie. Well, maybe a little bit. I was a slick hippie, a bit of a dandy. My dad never approved of what I wore or what I did, though. Later he would come down to our store in Gastown and tell me I had the wrong shoes on and that I should wear a suit to work.

The Sheppard's clothing store made no sense at all, of course. It was upstairs from the Sheppard Shoes store so nobody could find it unless they knew it was there. And a lot of people never bothered to find out. So, I guess you could say it was struggling. Then one day Peter told me he was thinking about going out on his own and wondered if I wanted to go with him. Why not? I thought. I had nothing else to do.

Peter found a location for the store he wanted to open and my dad offered to loan him some money— $13,500—to get started as long as he made me a 50 percent partner. I had no business skills, but I looked good and I dressed well, so Peter agreed. And so, in 1970, we signed a lease and Fox & Fluevog was born.

The car that I gave Peter Fox a ride to work in. 1953 MGTD John & Peter — yes I wore those suits to work!

1970

Around Christmas of 1969, John meets Peter Fox, manager of Sheppard Shoes, at his parents' church. In 1970, the two open a shoe store in historic Gastown. The partnership, known as Fox & Fluevog, lasts a decade.

Not long after Fox & Fluevog opens, international supermodel Kecia Nyman walks into the store and walks out with John's heart. Three months later, they're married, and John is hobnobbing with the jet set.

We celebrated with dinner at the Old Spaghetti Factory (which is still there, beside our existing flagship store).

Fox & Fluevog was a revolutionary shop in Vancouver, maybe in the world. It was located in a vintage building in the most historic part of the city, Gastown, a neigh-bourhood of cobblestone streets and brick low-rises that date back to the nineteenth century. It's named for a saloonkeeper, "Gassy Jack" Deighton. This is where the city began, but for a long time it was pretty rough—in the Dirty Thirties it was all warehouses and hobo camps; after the Second World War it was the city's skid row. Then in the 1960s, the city planned to put a freeway through here. That woke everyone up, and people began to realize how beautiful the old buildings were, and they decided to preserve them instead.

In the 1960s and '70s, Gastown was really interesting. It was really fun. It was revolutionary. It was that sense that we could change the world. Hippies, peaceniks and draft dodgers came to Vancouver from all over North America, and everyone hung out here. My first employee, Robert, lived in a commune, and they all had multiple partners. It's just the way it was back then. Gastown was filled with bars and pubs and boutiques, and I remember a hip vegetarian restaurant called the Aspidistra that used to play LGFM, the alternative radio station. Hip was different back then; it was a little hippier, a little grungier. There was lots of Grateful Dead. There was lots of pot, too, and other drugs. In 1971, a bunch of hippies held a "Grasstown Smoke-in," which was busted up by the cops—it became known as the Gastown riot, and it happened right outside our store.

They tell me now that I seemed so arrogant back then, but it was because I was insecure.

Anyway, Fox & Fluevog was really funky. It had these sixteen-foot ceilings, stylin' with all vintage and antique furniture and old books, thousands of them, that we bought for five cents a pop from the Opportunity Rehabilitation Workshop. The interior design was loosely based on the library scene in the 1938 movie *Pygmalion*.

Kecia & I in 1971 outside our first store

Director Robert Altman buys a knee-high boot while filming the movie *McCabe & Mrs. Miller* in Vancouver.

In August, after weeks of unrest, the Gastown riot breaks out right outside Fox & Fluevog.

John and Kecia travel to Mexico, where they discover a warehouse full of vintage children's shoes. They come back and sell them with the motto Brand-New 50-year-old Shoes.

And I used to come to work dressed up in this three-piece tweed suit with knickers and buckled shoes. I was, like, hot stuff, right? But I was never a flake. I was honest, I was hard-working and I was reliable. Peter needed that kind of stability.

It was my ego that got me. It took me out and she took me out.

When I started doing this, I knew what people were thinking and I knew how to tickle them. I wasn't all that smart in school, but I had more street smarts than most people. Emotional intelligence or whatever you call it. And I always understood women. I had a strong sense of my feminine side. And strangely, I ended up in this business where I make women feel happy. Makes sense, right?

Our shoes were expensive—we'd sell knee-high lace-up patent leather boots in five colours for men.

We started selling platforms. I had people flying up from LA to buy my shoes. I was the man, selling $270 boots for men. I suspect now that all my customers were doing something illegal. Gambling. Smuggling. Selling drugs. We talk about drugs in the neighbourhood now, but back then it really was the Wild West. Everyone was doing pot, hash, LSD, mushrooms, angel dust, you name it, but nobody knew what it would do to you. A lot of people went to jail and a lot of people died. We romanticize it now, but people forget: the '60s and '70s had their dark side, too.

Still, it was an exciting and fun time, with endless possibility.

Then one day, about six months after we opened, a woman named Kecia Nyman walked into the store. She was tall and blond and beautiful with big smoke-blue eyes. It took me a day to start dating her and three months to marry her. Over five years of craziness followed. It was my ego that got me. It took me out and she took me out.

Kecia was an international model with hundreds of magazine covers to her name, a superstar of the 1960s.

I Turned Peter into a dog in my first catogue!

Peter and John attend a hippie church and hire the street kids who attend services to make belts, bags and clogs in their Gastown store.

1972

She was part of the jet set—the big exciting world of glamour and money and creative people—and she introduced me to it. Even though she was eight years older than me, my father, my pastor and my business partner all encouraged me to marry her. We used the ring she'd been given by her ex, the actor Peter Sellers, for a down payment on a house in North Vancouver. How suburban, right? We got a cute dog named Freddy Fluevog. We had a son named Jonathan. We had it all, for a little while at least.

It was a refreshing time in a lot of ways, and a good time. For instance, there was the time we visited Mexico. In 1971, someone came into Fox & Fluevog and told us about these amazing antique shoes in a warehouse in Mexico City. I went down there with my extraordinary just-married wife and found these boxes of mostly baby shoes from the 1920s. We sold them all, like trinkets. But despite the myth everyone tells about us, they weren't actually part of our shoe stock.

Instead, Peter and I went to England and got our shoes made there with the help of people like George Cox. We'd go to shoe shows, and Peter would find a factory that he liked. Then we'd take the different

components of the shoes they produced and mess around with them, trying different colours and stitching and heel shapes, and get the shoes made the way we liked. I wouldn't call that designing, I'd call that line building. But we created unique shoes that you could only buy at Fox & Fluevog, like the knee-high boot that the director Robert Altman bought when he was in Vancouver filming the movie *McCabe & Mrs. Miller*, with Warren Beatty and Julie Christie.

Then there were the clogs. In 1972, we attended St. Margaret's Anglican, a charismatic hippie church near the Pacific National Exhibition grounds, where the street kids would go. We hired the kids to work in the shop and got them making belts and bags in the back of the store. Hiring hippies made us cool. Then Peter bought some shoe lasts from Spain (the forms around which a shoe is built), and we got them making clogs. The clogs were expensive—$75 a pair back in 1973— but they sold really well. We offered them in custom colours, with handmade flower details, and if they didn't quite fit someone, I'd wrap the clogs around their feet.

One of the people who joined us was Ken Rice. He was from Toronto and had dabbled in leather work,

our first store was like a Victorian living room.

Peter and John open a store on Granville Street that looks like an elaborate bedroom. This is followed by stores in Victoria and Edmonton and a third store in Vancouver, on West Broadway.

Jonathan Fluevog Jr. is born.

Peter and John become the first to sell Dr. Martens shoes in North America.

making belts and bags while studying at the Ontario College of Art. In 1970, he headed west on a one-way train ticket and, like me, met Peter at church. He started making bags and belts for us, and later he got into making clogs for us, too—beautiful, artistic clogs. By 1973, he had decided to become a traditional shoemaker.

Around then we began expanding. We opened Fox & Fluevog stores in Victoria and Edmonton and a second location in Vancouver, over on Granville Street. By the end of the 1970s, we had five or six shops. We even considered taking on a partner and opening stores across Canada. But it wasn't really the right energy, the right vibe or the right time.

Eventually Peter started designing his own lasts and his own designs. He became famous for his romantic Louis-heeled granny boots and later for medieval Tudor and Arts and Crafts–inspired shoes, as well as what he called his Adult Baby Shoe, which had a wedge heel built inside the shoe like Salvatore Ferragamo shoes had back in the 1930s. It was all very cool.

But it wasn't the direction I was going in back then.

So, here I was in the 1970s, thinking I'm the bomb. Why wouldn't I? I had everything I could have wanted. So of course it was just a matter of time before it all ended.

Five years after I married Kecia, our marriage was over. In 1977 we went our separate ways. It was hard. I thought we'd be together forever, but it didn't work out that way. Even though she made me crazy by the end of our time together, I can still picture that day she walked into my store and changed my life.

I didn't stay single very long, because I met Ingrid Sova, who worked in the store making clogs. She was bright and blond, strong and smart. We married and had two kids, Adrian and Britta, a home life and twenty great years together. But I'm getting ahead of myself.

The 1970s changed me, they changed Peter and they changed Vancouver, too. It was a decade of political, economic and cultural turmoil that transformed a pretty but rough logging town, nicknamed "Terminal City" for its place at the end of the railway line, into a modern metropolis that would become a model for

I'm still driving this car! Most days

John buys his 1948 Austin Dorset.

John hires a woman named Ingrid Sova, who would eventually play another important role in his life.

the rest of the world. It was a decade of protests and riots and activism that created powerful movements like Greenpeace.

By the end of the decade, though, a lot of that righteous momentum was gone. The economic boom was ending, thanks to high inflation and an ongoing energy crisis, and a recession was on the horizon. A lot of my customers were gone, too. There was a lot of drug abuse back then, and the kind of people who wouldn't think twice about spending $270 on a pair of boots also wouldn't think twice about breaking the law. Like Jimmy Mack. He was an imposing man with a stutter, who wore a big white hat with a feather, and he'd pull all this cash out of his sock. I don't know how he made his money, but it sure wasn't by doing anything legal. He's gone. A lot of my customers ended up killing themselves or being shot or dying of overdoses. All those young people who worked for us, their dreams and ideals, they were gone, too. The delusion ended.

And then Peter and I split. I bought him out and he moved to New York, where his shoes showed up in the pages of *Vogue* and on stage on Broadway and on the feet of every cool bride. For a while in the 1980s, you couldn't open a magazine without seeing an ad for Peter Fox Shoes. He's back in Vancouver, retired now, and I'll always be grateful to him. He showed me a path and a place to go. He gave me the road map.

Peter Fox showed me a path and a place to go. He gave me the road map.

In the 1970s when we started, I had no idea how cool the store was, particularly the handmade shoes we sold. It was really advanced, but I didn't know that. The store could have been anywhere in the world. Even in Italy. It would have been even more successful there.

I thought I could keep it going on my own. Why wouldn't I? Of course, I had no idea what was hurtling down the road at me. JF

John and Kecia divorce.

John marries Ingrid; they go on to have two children, Adrian in 1981 and Britta in 1983.

Peter sells his share of the company to John and heads to New York.

Peter was really tall back then! ha

1979

CELESTIAL INSPIRATION

Some people think angels descend from above to hand ideas to John. This is how he finds inspiration.

People often wonder where I get my ideas. Truth is, they come from everywhere. I don't follow trends. I don't want to do what everyone else is doing. Of course, trends sometimes find me anyway; sometimes an idea is just in the air and I can't ignore it. But mostly, I take note of what my mind wants me to see— a colour, a shape, a fragrance, a sound, a story, a place, a person, a dream—and then I turn it into a shoe. But there are three things that will always inspire me: spirituality, cars and fashion.

PREVIOUS PAGE In 2018, artist Thomaz Magno created this epic tapestry immortalizing key memories from John's life. Take a magnifying glass and see how many you can spot.

SPIRITUALITY

MY JOURNEY ON THIS PLANET —my work, my family, my life— has been my spiritual journey. I like mystery. I like to think there are underlying mysteries to what we do and how we interact with each other. I hope that my faith and my spirituality is a good idea and it doesn't hurt anybody. It does some good in my life and to those around me. It just is.

When I was growing up, my family was very religious, but it wasn't a creative spirit that moved them. I've since learned that God inspires creativity, that we can all be incredibly creative when we join in and listen. It isn't any supernatural thing. It's available to all of us. Communicate to the Creator and creation follows. Experiencing that is the essence of who we should be because it draws us into community. We need to train ourselves to watch and listen.

At the lowest points in my life, when I thought I'd lost everything, there was always someone who lifted me up, and it has taught me to let go and have faith.

You could say my shoes walk in the spirit of God or the Creator.

After all, Angel soles resist Satan. There are Urban Angels, Turbo Angels and Guardian Angels, as well as angels embedded in the wedge heels of the Wendy, a shoe named for a woman who died too young, but not before completing her mission on Earth. Other shoes have spirit-boosting names like Wonder, Promise, Peacemaker, Vow and Balthazar, named for a Wise Man with enough faith for three. And our shoes do good, too, raising money for charitable causes that are close to my heart.

I've always had a sense of good and evil. Evil is something that tears down goodness. Evil is something that tears down the light. Evil is something that lies and tells you something is true when it's not. It's evil not to think that you are made perfectly because you are. It's evil to think that other people are better than you. It's evil to put other people down to make yourself feel better. It's evil not to love yourself for who you are.

Goodness is the opposite of all that. Can we capture that feeling in a shoe? I don't know, but I can certainly try.

HERE'S THE KEY TO THE NUMBERS ON JOHN'S TAPESTRY (PREVIOUS PAGE):

01 The sign from Luxury Freeze, John's father's ice cream drive-in

02 The Sea Angel

03 A Flunicorn

04 John's bicycle

05 Fluebodies ad campaign

06 John's car, The Fluevog

07 Jack White in the Jack

08 Lady Gaga in the Cubist Cupcake

09 The Fluevocette

10 Fluevog's Crit Nasty Girls

11 Lady Miss Kier in the original Munster

12 Beyoncé in the Celestial Communication Seraphina

13 The Fluevogian Elves

14 #Voghead

15 Fluevog HQ office dogs, Pipo, Peanut & Adeline (not pictured: Otis!)

16 Mrs. Ruth Fluevog (she's wonderful)

17 John's first ever shoe design, the Truth Pilgrim

18 Fluevog's flagship store in Gastown, Vancouver

19 The Vogbot

20 John's 1948 Austin Dorset

"When I conjure John Fluevog Shoes in my mind, I see a '50s Hudson Hornet crossed with a Jaguar Mark X... in heels."

GAI GHERARDI,
EYEWEAR DESIGNER,
CO-FOUNDER, L.A.EYEWORKS

CARS

ANYONE WILL TELL YOU: when I'm not thinking about shoes, I'm thinking about cars.

Right now, I think I have six cars, in varying states of disrepair and reconstruction. I like mechanical things like this mechanical whirligig we've got in the Amsterdam store, moving shoes around in the window.

Cars are not status symbols to me. I like them because they have cool shapes and lines. I like them because they're a little bit different. To me, they're pieces of metal that move and express a feeling.

Cars have been part of my life since I was a little kid. My dad was really into cars, too, and I must have got that passion from him. Somewhere there's a picture of me as a three-year-old, sitting on the fender of his car, I think it was a Hillman. When he owned the Luxury Freeze, back in the late 1950s and early '60s, everyone would come to the drive-in to show off their cars. There were lots of custom cars, personalized with paint jobs and accessories like dingle balls and whitewall tires. I loved the lines of the cars, but I also loved the way you could make something uniquely your own with just a few little touches.

I'm a bit of a nerd when it comes to cars. I love the technical details. I never really liked the status cars, though. In high school, everyone had hot rods and I didn't have one. It didn't seem cool. I've had a Ferrari, but I felt weird driving it. I've always been more into cars like the Citroën ID I drove to California in 1969. It was a space age–looking car with a suspension that moved up and down, like the DS. It was completely not a teenage car. It was not cool in any way whatsoever. But maybe that's typical of me. Maybe I'm a little eccentric. I liked it because it was a little weird. You know: no one else has one, so I'll have that, please.

Then there's the white 1948 Austin Dorset I've had since 1973. I like that car because it's so non-cool. It's cool because it's not cool. The Dorset is a two-door saloon made by Austin in the 1940s, right after the war. They also made the Devon, which had four doors. These cars were a funky mix of old and new. They looked old-fashioned, even back then, but they had hydraulic brakes, modern bodies and coil-sprung independent suspensions. Wherever I've moved, I've kept the Austin all these years.

Most of all, though, I love Jaguars. They have the lines I like. It was a Jag I sold to finance my store in Seattle, and I'm right now redesigning a 1951 Jaguar Mark V Drophead. I've been wanting to redesign a car for a while, and this one has the shape I wanted.

It's not the first car I've Fluevoged, though. That would be The Fluevog. My dad bought this Jaguar Mark X back in 1966. When he died in 1995, I bought the car from his estate. It was in such bad shape, most sensible people would have written it off without a second thought. It was such a beautiful car, though, I decided to bring her back to life. I could see the glory within her. But I couldn't resist making a few changes.

I ended up completely redesigning the car, inside and out. I rebuilt the frame, installed a V-8 engine, transformed the interior with faux crocodile leather and lowered the roof. Yes, I chopped a classic Jaguar. It took me two years, but I ended up with one of the most original Fluevogs ever to strike the street. You can't miss it—she's the car with the stitching on the side.

You know, it really is true what they say. When I'm drawing a shoe, I'm thinking about a car. When I'm drawing a car, I'm thinking about a shoe. My team calls it the Fluevog Continuum.

"Baroque yet countercultural, comfortably klutzy yet streamlined Mod, Fluevog is a welcome anomaly."

LINDA DYETT,
NEW YORK FASHION
JOURNALIST

FASHION

FASHION IS A FEELING. It's a feeling that gives people confidence. And it's amazing how important that feeling is to some people.

Some people say my shoes are anti-fashion. It's true, they don't follow trends, though sometimes they meet trends halfway. Fashionistas often don't like my shoes. They want to fit in and don't want to risk looking different from the crowd. But I don't use fashion as a way of fitting in. I use it as a way of being an individual. Your own weird self is OK. And Fluevogers love looking different. They love marching to their own trombone.

Just because we don't follow trends doesn't mean we're not affected by fashion, though.

Fashion is like anything. It's like a spirit or emotion that runs through the world or atmosphere and people catch it. It's there to be caught. I'll be doing a look and inevitably, there will be someone else doing it, too. I'm sure that even happened to Mozart. These feelings and emotions that run through our society at different times and in different places are there to be harvested and used if one is sensitive to them.

Take the last couple of years. There's been a sense of impending doom. Maybe it's the natural disasters or politics or the economy or the anger on social media. But the mood has been apocalyptic. For Fall 2018, I was inspired by medieval armour and silhouettes, *Mad Max*, the original 1980s Thunderdome and steam-punk.

I've always had a sense of what's cool and what's not. I'm aware of my presence and what I put out there. How it makes me feel and how it makes other people feel. I'm aware of the feelings and emotions around me. It's not a big deal to me. It just is. It's the ability, like anybody that's artistically inclined, to watch and see.

I've been through a lot of fashion eras, and I caught the fever of what was going on at the time, but I never really became any of those eras.

When I was a kid, hanging around the Luxury Freeze, it was scene central and fashion was part of the scene. The coolest people drove the coolest cars and wore the coolest clothes. By the time I was in junior high, I wore black kicks because that was the thing to wear. I wore them with white socks, a button-up shirt and Levi's jeans, tight and short.

Later in the 1960s, when I was in high school, my big focus was girls. I chased them, I talked to them, I loved them and they occasionally loved me. How I dressed became important.

I was a trendy teenager. I was noticeable. I was the cool kid, even though I always felt inadequate because I was so bad at school. Even then I could sense how every season things changed, how the vibe changed in fashion and cars.

As I mentioned, when we opened Fox & Fluevog in 1970, I'd go to work in a three-piece tweed suit with knickers, knee-high hose and shoes with buckles on them. I was a hippie dandy. Later in the 1970s, I wore the flare pants, florals and see-through shirts of the disco era. Did it become my persona? No. I didn't want to be that. I wanted to *watch* that.

In the 1980s, I'd wear bold colours, big shoulders and shiny fabrics. In the 1990s, well, grunge wasn't my thing, and by then, I was confident enough to wear what I liked. What I like is something comfortable, but a little bit offbeat, oversized or asymmetrical, with some unusual flair, like maybe some purple socks or a natty scarf wrapped around my neck.

I like things that look good. I like the look and feel of lines. I like how lines make a person feel. The ability to see things, I think we as humans all have it. We just have it in degrees. I was always OK with wearing something out of sync, as long as it looked good. After all, why would I want to look like anyone else? And why would you?

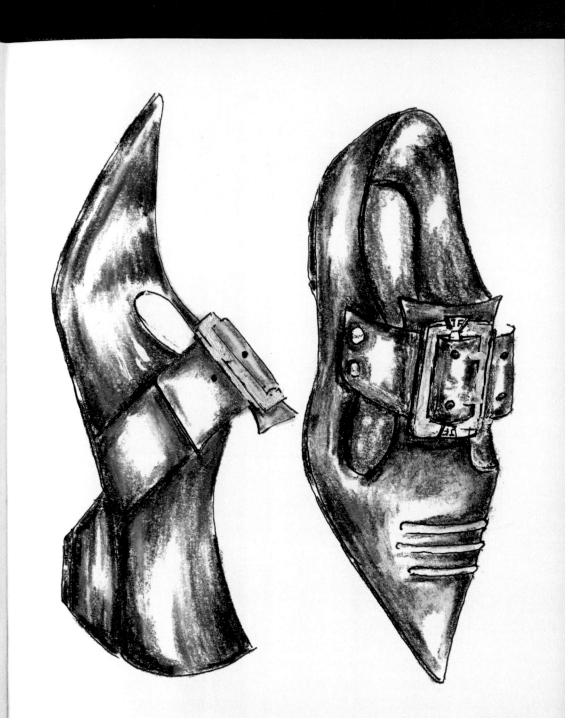

In the 1980s, punk gives way to New Wave and then to grunge, and Vogs are the chosen footwear of cool cats no matter how they rock. Things are challenging for a neophyte businessman in the midst of a global recession. But John finds kindred spirits who help him tell his story. Most importantly, he discovers his inner artist.

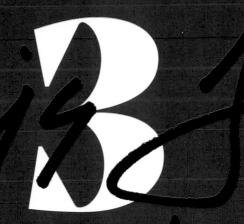

F is for

all things

THE
PILGRIM
1980–1989

that give

hope

IN THE 1980S, things got tough for me. Things were tough for a lot of people. There was a big recession going on, with high inflation and interest rates that shot up to 21 percent. But I was also struggling with learning how to run a business and, of course, dealing with my own self-doubt. By the end of the decade, my business had completely transformed, and so had I.

So it's 1980. Peter had decided he wanted to get out of the partnership and he sold me the stores, which turned out to be good timing for him, but not so great for me. Business was already starting to slow down when the recession hit.

I was bombing along, doing what Peter did, or at least I thought I was. But he'd been doing the buying, and he had the relationships with the factories in England. And I didn't really know how to run a business. Over the next five, six years, I had to learn how to do the buying and everything. I almost went bankrupt twice. By 1985 I had closed all the stores except two in Vancouver—Granville Street and West Broadway. Even the Gastown store was gone and it would be more than twenty years before I could return to my old neighbourhood. Business was hard and things were looking tough, even though

I had what should have been the silver bullet to success: the shoe brand all the cool kids craved.

Back around 1973, 1974, Peter and I had started carrying Dr. Martens shoes. I think we were the first in Canada, maybe North America, to bring them in. They were already popular in the 1970s among a certain clientele, especially in the UK. But in the 1980s, with punk and New Wave and then grunge, they just exploded. They became the footwear of the music scene. And we were the ones that had them.

The familiar heavy black shoes with yellow stitching were designed for workers. Police officers wore them, and factory workers, and later, punks. Those punks picked up on them and wore them as a rebellious gesture. No one dreamed that Docs would become what they became.

It's important to know that what made it a Dr. Martens shoe wasn't the way it looked, it was its patented construction process. It was, in fact, its sole. I took that sole and began making what I thought were interesting shoes with uppers in cool colours and fabrics like leopard-print pony hair. Customers loved them so much that 60 to 70 percent of my inventory had those soles.

1980

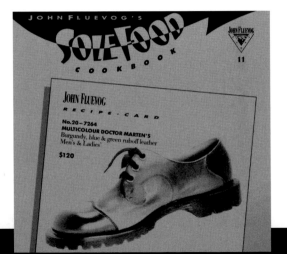

The Fox & Fluevog partnership had ended, although the name stays, for now at least. John's first stand-alone store is on Granville Street, just up from the famous Commodore Ballroom.

The partnership ended fairly well. We're still friends

I eventually realized that wasn't a good idea because I wanted to sell John Fluevog shoes, not Dr. Martens shoes. I also found out that Docs had PVCs in them. That's what makes them stick and wear so well, but it's not so great for the environment. So I knew we'd have to part ways. If I hadn't made the move, they could have cut me out anyway.

Meanwhile, in 1983, I'd connected with a guy named Dave Webber. Dave is a graphic artist and a writer, and he was right in step with Fluevog. He started designing these cool little catalogues for us. At first, they were just that, catalogues of our product lineup with prices and descriptions. But then I started coming up with themes, some of them pretty far out, with stories and illustrations that weren't always just of the shoes. With that direction, he then turned me into something of a mythical character. These weren't flyers, they were actually zines. Do you remember zines? They were these funky little independent mags you'd get in the 1980s, big with the punk and New Wave kids. They were really cool.

Punk had been a thing in the UK since the mid-1970s. It was as much about class rebellion as it was a reaction against the music scene of the 1960s. By 1978, Vancouver had its own scene with bands like D.O.A., Pointed Sticks and the Subhumans. Kids in dyed green Mohawks were hanging around on Granville Street, just like the hippies had done in Gastown a decade earlier. Punk became New Wave and post-punk and all those other anarchic movements, and then by the mid-1980s, grunge had started to emerge from Seattle. It was a powerful fashion moment, and I was right in the thick of it.

I almost went bankrupt twice. By 1985 I had closed all stores except two in Vancouver.

The Dr. Martens I was selling were *the* footwear of punk and grunge. I should have had it made. Instead, I was running out of money and, for a while at least, it seemed I was at a dead end.

DAve and John passing the buck.

After years of soaring inflation, unemployment and fuel prices, interest rates skyrocket to 21 percent. The recession makes it a difficult time to be a retailer selling shoes that are not in step with the ordinary. But John's financial struggles are just beginning.

Adrian Fluevog is born.

John had been selling Dr. Martens since the 1970s, but in the 1980s he goes wild with signature embellishments—like pink pony hair or leopard-print uppers—that New Wave club kids love.

Britta Fluevog is born.

John Fluevog connects with Dave Webber, a talented graphic artist and writer who captures his quirky mission in funky zine-like catalogues. They work together for more than twenty years.

1981   **1982**   **1983**

It was 1985. I was down to two retail stores in Vancouver. I owed the bank $100,000, which exceeded my total inventory. By accounting standards, I was bankrupt. I was also supporting two small kids, a teenager and a mortgage. It wasn't a good combination to say the least.

high debt NOT recommended! but I did get through.

The Broadway store was losing $5,000 a month and the Granville store was making $5,000 a month. I knew I'd have to close the Broadway store, but if I did, I would limit my options for buying product. Besides, owning just one store didn't sound like a fun career move.

Opening a new store in Alberta was out—the recession was even worse there than in BC, and I'd just closed the store in Edmonton. But what about Seattle? It was only a two-and-a-half-hour drive south of Vancouver and offered a whole new market.

So I hopped into my fancy E-Type Jaguar, the only asset I owned outright, and drove down to Seattle. I walked around for a few hours and then, right near Pike Place Market, I found a great little shop with a For Rent sign in the window. A month later I was the proud new tenant of that space. (I think the Jag helped give me street cred.)

I hired a contractor to start work on the Seattle store and held a closing sale at the Broadway location. I was still on the hook for the remainder of the lease there, but luckily, someone came by and bought some of the lights and other fixtures, and actually took over the lease.

Meanwhile, I was wondering how to get my remaining inventory across the border. Technically, because of the loan, the bank owned the inventory, and I was pretty sure they wouldn't like me moving it out of the country. But I reasoned that if I didn't do it, the bank had little chance of being paid back anyway.

And then there was the question of how I would pay the contractor. I still remember the exact Vancouver street corner I was driving past where it hit me that

Would you buy shoes from this man?

Desperate to keep his struggling business afloat, John closes all but two stores, both in Vancouver.

From May to October, Expo 86 brings the world to Vancouver. John sells his E-type Jaguar to open a boutique near Seattle's Pike Place Market. The gamble takes off: the store is an instant success. He renames the business: John Fluevog Shoes.

In November, John meets a spiritual figure named Augustine who convinces John to start designing his own shoes and, more importantly, to sign them. The F-sole is born.

I could sell my car to pay for the renovations. Problem solved. I put an ad in the paper and, after a month of no response, a gentleman showed up, gave me a $500 deposit, and disappeared. Three weeks later, on the morning of the very day I had to pay the contractor, the buyer came by with a cheque for the balance owing on the car. It worked out to the exact amount needed for the shop renovations. Talk about serendipity! I personally delivered the payment that afternoon.

Meanwhile, Vancouver was throwing a coming-of-age party for the city's centennial: the World Exposition on Transportation and Communication, better known as Expo 86. Between May 2, when Prince Charles and Princess Diana opened the fair, and October 13, when the last pavilion closed, more than 22 million people attended. The world had finally discovered Vancouver.

For the most part, I was too busy to join the party. That summer, I loaded all the shoes and shelves and chairs from the Broadway store into a rented truck and headed back across the border. At customs, I discovered I could discount the inventory as used, and was reimbursed the duty I'd paid when the stock entered Canada, which amounted to $10,000. Things were looking up.

The Seattle store opened in August 1986. Along with the new location, we had a new name: no longer Fox & Fluevog, but John Fluevog Shoes. It was the beginning of the grunge movement and I was selling shoes that Seattle had never seen before. And right away I started to sell shoes, like, boom!

But after the initial euphoria of increased sales, November arrived and sales dropped. It shouldn't have come as a surprise given that I was already running low on inventory when I opened the store, but the reality hit hard. I had been in survival mode for so long and now it felt like I was at square one. Again.

One miserable, rainy November day I told my wife how drained I was, physically and emotionally, by the financial ups and downs of the business. Maybe it was time to find another source of income, I said. Maybe it was time to quit. It was a relief to say it out loud.

Later that same morning, I received a phone call from a close friend who told me he was sending someone I needed to meet down to my office. An hour or so later, in walks Augustine, a Mexican-American guy sporting a mullet, tight jeans and cowboy boots, looking like he had just stepped out of a jacked-up 1978 Ford Torino.

The first shoes I designed a proud Papa!

NO.9/ BLACK LEATHER
WHITE LEATHER
THE "PILGRIM" UOSHOE—
YOUR ROOTS OF FASHION.
WOMEN'S
115—

Augustine, I guess you'd call him an itinerant seer. He was not a minister, but he had a spiritual gift. He could see things no one else could. He could see them in me. But I didn't know that right away, and I was pretty skeptical that he had anything to offer.

I started to tell Augustine a bit about my business, but he silenced me and waved me to my chair. Then he declared, "God does not want you to quit your business." How did he know I'd been thinking just that? He told me he saw me surrounded by shoes, really crazy shoes, and they were all over the world, in different countries. It sounds strange, but even then it felt like truth.

He told me my name would be powerful and well recognized. Then he looked at me and said, "What's your name?" I told him, and he said, "Put your name on all your shoes." So Augustine was the guy who told me to put the F on the bottom of all my shoes. "Kids love that *F* thing," he said. That's how I came up with my F-soles, and I still sell them today. Who knew, right?

I think it's fair to say that if I had not accepted Augustine's words, I would not have pushed forward through all the hardships of the next few years. God knew exactly what I needed to hear. It was like He knew I was a wuss and needed someone to come along and hit me over the head.

I used Augustine as a sounding board for years. Without his encouragement, I wouldn't have been able to transition to designing and making my own shoes, because I didn't have a clue how to do it. I was just a shoe retailer. Becoming a designer was a big shift in my thinking.

He told me he saw me surrounded by shoes, really crazy shoes.

A lot of people already assumed I was the designer, because my name was on the store and the shoes we were selling were unlike anything they'd ever seen. But I'd never considered myself creative. I never knew how to design anything. As I said before, I used to think artists were sketchy, and I certainly never saw myself as one. But then I thought, actually, I can do this. And so I just did.

Did this come true?

Fluevog Shoes opens in Boston.

John designs the Munster, a glamorous platform shoe with a big, sexy heel and dramatic buckle.

Fluevog Shoes opens on Toronto's Queen Street.

John introduces the Swordfish with its narrow, pointy toe complete with toe bump. Alice Cooper rocks it for decades.

One day in 1986 I saw a customer in the street and she was wearing a pair of cowboy boots with the toes turned up. It was really punk and I loved it. And I thought, wouldn't that make a great shoe? I started sketching a shoe with a pointy Western toe and a big buckle and a flat heel, because I didn't know how to design a heel. It was the first shoe I drew the design for. I called it the Pilgrim because of the buckle and it kind of looked like a pilgrim shoe. It wasn't any more complicated than that.

I not only drew the shoe, I made the last—the form that the shoe is built around—and the pattern, then gave it to Ken Rice. He made the first Pilgrims by hand here in Vancouver, although later I had them produced at a factory in England. And it worked! That made me trust myself more. So, in 1988, I did it again.

This time I made the prototype myself from plaster of Paris in my basement. I remember it was this big blob, wet and dripping everywhere. Eventually I had a cast that was usable and I took it to the factory in England. There were some raised eyebrows when they saw what I wanted to make, but they made it anyway. When one of the factory girls saw it, she said, "Wow, that's a monster shoe!" Only with her accent it sounded like "munster."

And so it became the Munster, and that shoe changed everything for me.

One of the factories we worked with even hired me to design some shoes for them when their designer, Terry de Havilland, who was famous for his glam 1970s platforms, suddenly left. I asked them to put my name on the shoes in lieu of payment, and that's how my name became known from Iceland to Australia. Don't forget, as far as fashion was concerned, Vancouver didn't exist. It wasn't even on the map until Expo 86. Getting my name out there was way more important than earning a few bucks.

And business started to take off. I started selling shoes wholesale. I opened a store on Newbury in Boston just to see if I could. Now I'm probably the longest lasting retailer on that strip, a little kid from Vancouver. I opened a store in Toronto. Then I opened a store in New York and Fluevog became synonymous with coolness in Soho. I could get into any club and all the super-trendy people worked for me. It was so fun!

As the decade ended, on the surface, I looked like Tom Terrific. Underneath, though, I was still insecure dyslexic John. But it would take a few more years before everything came crashing down again. **JF**

looking as handsome as ever!

1989

No.54

No.45

No.55

No.52

CATALOGUES OF COOL

Not just shopping guides, these little zines told the story of Fluevog in witty ways.

No.47

No.48

No.49

COLORS AVAILABLE $149 •No.56-JESSICA T-STRAP PLAT-
FORM: ASK ABOUT THE COLORS AVAILABLE $149

ULE: BLACK

•No.65-833

From 1980 right up until the mid-2000s, one of the ways we spread the word of Fluevog was through our catalogues. These were small pamphlets, no bigger than the palm of your hand, and only a few pages long. They started as collections of black-and-white sketches of shoes with descriptions and prices. But thanks to the quirky genius of our good friend graphic artist Dave Webber, and others, they quickly became much more than just a sales tool. They were really zines that told the story of what was happening in the world of Fluevog.

PREVIOUS PAGE The 1990s were the heyday of the catalogues, including this one titled "Sing and Dance Around the World."

the 7 Powers of Fluevogdom

JOHN FLUEVOG SHOES

unique soles for unique souls

Zines have been around since the 1940s, the evolution of traditional magazines and fanzines, but have their roots in political pamphlets that go back centuries. Traditionally, zines had a handmade vibe. They were independent in voice and small in circulation, with an offbeat, low-tech design aesthetic. Graphically, they

had a lot in common with movements like Dada and Surrealism. They were big with subcultures like sci-fi fans and punk rockers. They were perfect for us.

The Fluevog catalogues were punny and funny. They connected our people and our shoes. And they introduced the famous Fluevog catchphrases, many of which we still

use today: "Unique soles for unique souls." "Don't delay, Fluevog today." "Angel powered and Satan resistant." "No one is tougher than an Angel." "Let the un-brainwashing begin." "Celebrate your body, but for God's sake don't worship it."

Let's take a trippy trip back into the past…

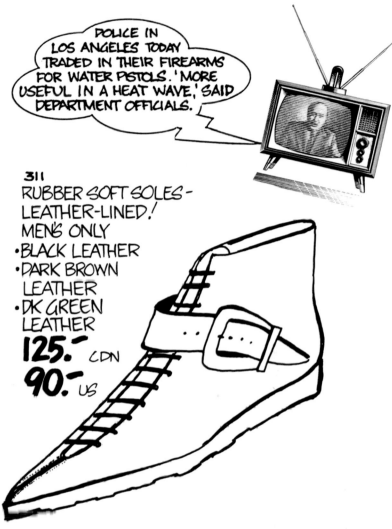

RIGHT HERE AT HOME, PANDEMONIUM REIGNS AS THERE'S DANCING IN THE STREETS.

POLICE IN LOS ANGELES TODAY TRADED IN THEIR FIREARMS FOR WATER PISTOLS. 'MORE USEFUL IN A HEAT WAVE,' SAID DEPARTMENT OFFICIALS.

309
ROCK 'N ROLL'S NARROW TOES – BUT NOT SUPER POINTS!
WOMEN'S ONLY
• BLACK SUEDE/BLACK LEATHER
• BLACK/OCELOT TOPS
79.⁻ CDN
56.⁻ US

310
SHERIFF'S NARROW SQUARED-OFF TOES WITH A WESTERN BUCKLE!
MEN'S ONLY
89.⁻ CDN
65.⁻ US

BLACK
BLACK/WHITE TOPS

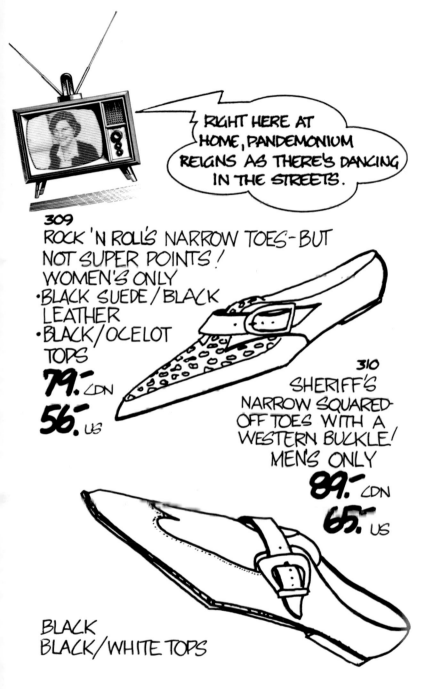

311
RUBBER SOFT SOLES – LEATHER-LINED!
MEN'S ONLY
• BLACK LEATHER
• DARK BROWN LEATHER
• DK GREEN LEATHER
125.⁻ CDN
90.⁻ US

Catalogues as sales tool

First and foremost, the catalogues were designed to sell shoes. We'd gather all the designs in the pages of the catalogues, with cheeky descriptions and, of course, prices and an order form. Sometimes we'd have a theme, like 1986's headline-grabbing "The National Shoes," the penny-pinching "Bang for Your Buck Book" or 1994's fall catalogue: "Stepping Out and Moving On Up to a Higher Plane—Styling All the Way."

OPEN
SOURCE
FOOTWEAR

IS YOUR IMAGINATION ahead of the whole shoe industry and you're sick of waiting for them to catch up? Here's your chance to go over their heads and deal with someone who actually cares what you want. All that you need is that brilliant idea. Even just for part of a shoe — scribble it down and tack it on the board. We don't care if it's on a bar napkin, as long as we can make it out. So, fax it, mail it, email it, bring it in, just get it to us!

DESIGNED WITH REAL FLUEVOGERS *opensourcefootwear.com*

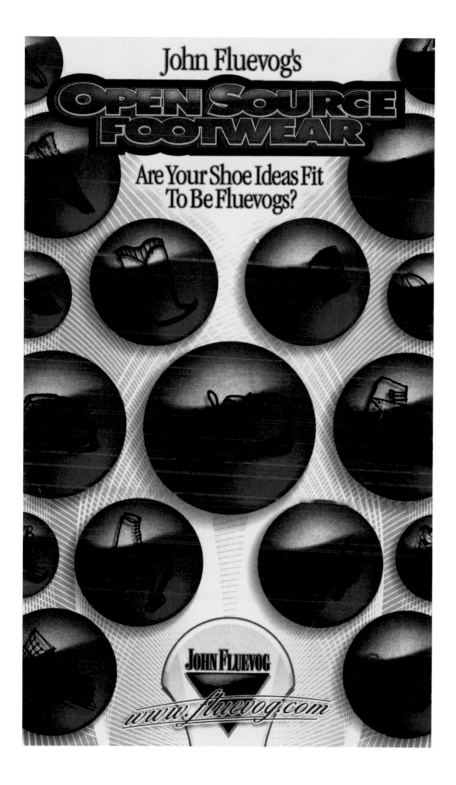

The Open Source Footwear program encouraged Fluevogers to draw their own dream shoes.

Fox&Fluevog
Shoe Template

....
your shoe name   *designed by*

We also used the catalogues to introduce Fluevogers to innovations like, for instance, the concept of Open Source Footwear, which allowed them to have a say in the design of their shoes. In that case, old and new technology came together in a way that could only be Fluevogian.

Catalogues as spiritual guide

Spirituality has always been integral to the Fluevog brand, and elements of faith, redemption, sin, virtue, enlightenment, angels, God and Satan all found their way into the pages of the catalogues. In 1999, a catalogue announced, "John Fluevog takes time for your sole." The 2003 "Book of Choice" paid homage to "the wordly word" and "the angelic angle" and featured shoes with names such as Halo, Good Boy and Future Angel. Others offered guides to goodness— "How to Get to Cloud 9"—and evil— "John Fluevog's Guide to Sin." One even suggested that John Fluevog himself had been kidnapped by Satan. (Perhaps that's why there was a rumour around Seattle that I was a Satanist.) And 2004's "Seven Powers of Fluevogdom," a paean to gratitude if ever there was one, was filled with hopeful shoe names (Freedom, Love and Choice) and loving homilies including "No man stands taller than he who is standing for someone else."

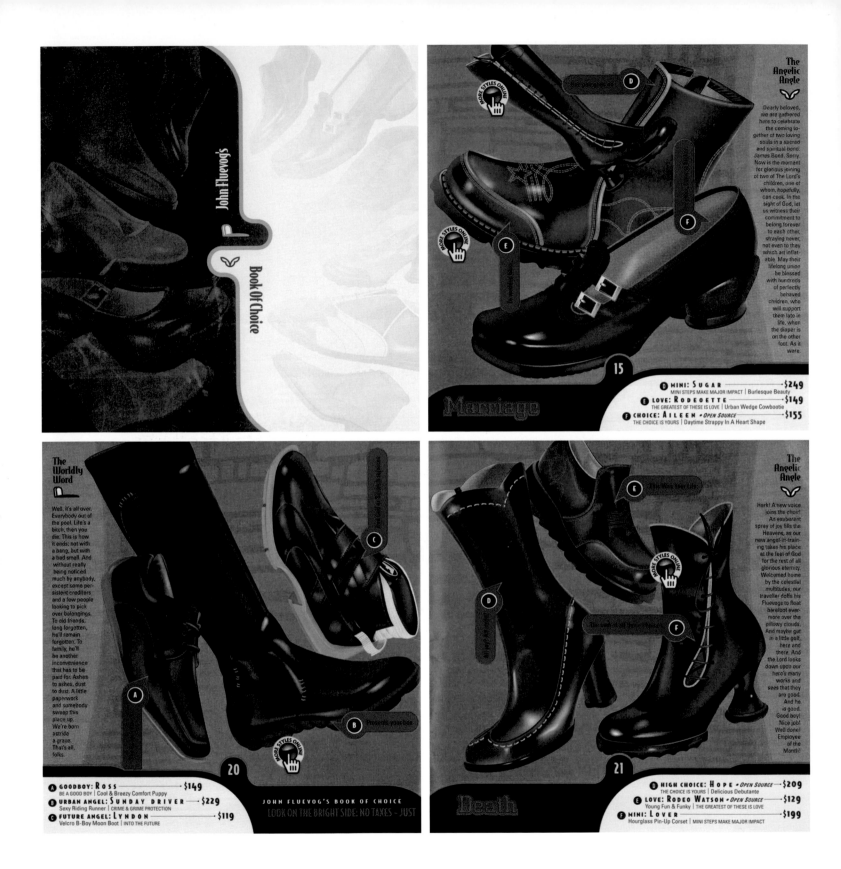

John Fluevog's

Book Of Choice

Dearly beloved, we are gathered here to celebrate the coming together of two loving souls in a sacred and spiritual bond. James Bond. Sorry. Now is the moment for glorious joining of two of The Lord's children, one of whom, hopefully, can cook. In the sight of God, let us witness their commitment to belong forever to each other, straying never, not even to they which art inflatable. May their lifelong union be blessed with hundreds of perfectly behaved children, who will support them late in life, when the diaper is on the other foot. As it were.

15

Marriage

D **MINI:** S U G A R — **$249**
MINI STEPS MAKE MAJOR IMPACT | Burlesque Beauty

E **LOVE:** R O D E O E T T E — **$149**
THE GREATEST OF THESE IS LOVE | Urban Wedge Cowbootie

F **CHOICE:** A I L E E N • *OPEN SOURCE* — **$155**
THE CHOICE IS YOURS | Daytime Strappy In A Heart Shape

The Worldly Word

Well, it's all over. Everybody out of the pool. Life's a bitch, then you die. This is how it ends; not with a bang, but with a bad smell. And without really being noticed much by anybody, except some persistent creditors and a few people looking to pick over belongings. To old friends, long forgotten, he'll remain forgotten. To family, he'll be another inconvenience that has to be paid for. Ashes to ashes, dust to dust. A little paperwork and somebody sweep this place up. We're born astride a grave. That's all, folks.

20

A **GOODBOY:** R O S S — **$149**
BE A GOOD BOY | Cool & Breezy Comfort Puppy

B **URBAN ANGEL:** S U N D A Y D R I V E R — **$229**
Sexy Riding Runner | CRIME & GRIME PROTECTION

C **FUTURE ANGEL:** L Y N D O N — **$119**
Velcro B-Boy Moon Boot | INTO THE FUTURE

JOHN FLUEVOG'S BOOK OF CHOICE
LOOK ON THE BRIGHT SIDE: NO TAXES - JUST

The Angelic Angle

Hark! A new voice joins the choir! An exuberant spray of joy fills the Heavens, as our new angel-in-training takes his place at the feet of God for the rest of all glorious eternity. Welcomed home by the celestial multitudes, our traveller doffs his Fluevogs to float barefoot evermore over the pillowy clouds. And maybe get in a little golf, here and there. And the Lord looks down upon our hero's many works and sees that they are good. And he is good. Good boy! Nice job! Well done! Employee of the Month!

21

Death

D **HIGH CHOICE:** H O P E • *OPEN SOURCE* — **$209**
THE CHOICE IS YOURS | Delicious Debutante

E **LOVE:** R O D E O W A T S O N • *OPEN SOURCE* — **$129**
Young Fun & Funky | THE GREATEST OF THESE IS LOVE

F **MINI:** L O V E R — **$199**
Hourglass Pin-Up Corset | MINI STEPS MAKE MAJOR IMPACT

Catalogues of John's life

The catalogues were a collaboration. I'd come up with the themes, as often as not channelling something that was going on in my life, and Dave Webber designed most of them. If I started recycling, we'd end up with 1993's "King John the Biodegradable." If I mused about safe sex, we'd get "The Complete Book of Fluevogian Safety," with photos of Safety Vog steel-toed boots accompanied by strictures on "safety against nerds" and "safety against general boredom."

I needed money and didn't want to go out of business, so we had "The Bank of John Fluevog." "Spend your savings account wisely," we urged. "I need the cash!" My love of cars rolled into an issue called "Travel in Style." And in 1990, we celebrated the twentieth anniversary of Fluevog with a capsule history and the memorable line: "Don't delay, Fluevog today."

Catalogues as community

The catalogues didn't just sell shoes, they created a sense of community. It was a certain type of person who got a kick out of the Fluevogian humour, and the catalogues catered to them with quirky zodiacs, helpful advice ("John Fluevog talks to young people about sex") and uplifting encouragement ("You are a superstar!" This is one of my themes— I believe we are all superstars.).

bandaid
$89

The healthy soles of Nurse Fluevog will help make you a vibrant star.

pill
$95

SUPERSTAR

Grand National

GN shoe
$180

GN boot
$269

SUPERSTAR

First through the gate and right on track
women's sizes only

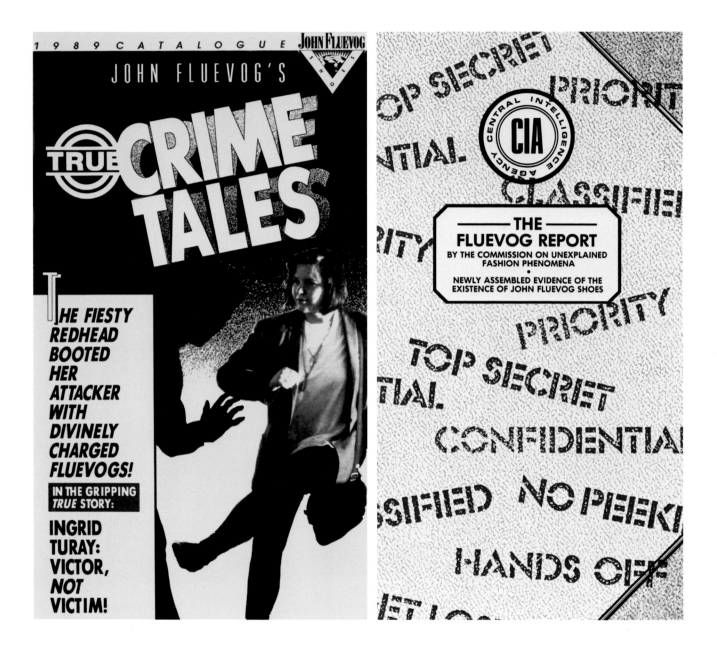

Perhaps the most compelling issue was John Fluevog's "True Crime Tales of 1989," which featured a letter from an intrepid Fluevoger named Ingrid Turay. The young woman was mugged in the street one day and used the pointy toes of her Pilgrim shoes to fend off her attacker. As she wrote, "I proceeded to kick the shit out of him until the police arrived."

CENTRAL INTELLIGENCE AGENCY

THE MOST TRUSTED NAME IN FOREIGN AND DOMESTIC ESPIONAGE.
JUST LOOK FOR THE BIG NEON EYE ON INTERSTATE 9
"OPEN 24 HOURS / REASONABLE RATES"

MEMO: *All Agents*
SUBJECT: *Reported sightings of John Fluevog Shoes*
PRIORITY: 1

High level communications express concern over the
spread of unexplained fashion phenomena known to
initiates as "Fluevoging".

Research indicates that growing numbers of people
in select groups are undergoing psychologically
challenging experiences through the use of special
devices applied to the feet. Reported characteristics
of such experiences include: the feeling of removal
from the everyday world; a heightened sense of general
well-being, self worth and purpose; radical change in
personal appearance; inreased clarity of vision &
the ability to fly, or at least dance really well.

Although sightings are becoming numerous, verbal
descriptions of the above devices have as yet
failed to produce any one truly exemplary specimen.
Our inside team, however, has now managed to obtain
actual microfilm photographs of the devices. Blowups
of these microfilms are supplied herein for your
perusal, numbered and with all pertinent information.
This matter must be subject to the earliest possible
investigation. You are expected to memorize this
information and act accordingly.

Your private orders may be found at the rear of
this book

CIA

15783

No.5/ "THE CHOSEN"
With cross
Black leather,
Red cross.
Women's.
CDN. $89
US $68

No.6/ "THE CHOSEN"
Plain pump
Black leather or
Black patent.
Women's.
CDN. $85
US $65

15783

No.8/ DERBY BOOT
Dr. Marten's Sole
Black leather,
Men's.
CDN. $145
US $120

No.26/ "DANDY"
Square toe
Black leather,
Women's.
CDN. $85
US $72

No.27/ "VINTAGE"
Lace boot
Black or brown suede,
Green nubuck
Women's.
CDN. $115
US $85

No.28/ "VINTAGE"
Slip-on
Black or
Red suede
Women's.

From the damp rainforests of the Pacific Northwest emerges a hard-rocking musical movement called grunge. Its uniform is the flannel shirt and John Fluevog Angel boots. As the decade progresses, grunge meets hip hop and techno, and Vogs rock the world from the office to the mosh pit to the rave dance floor. John gets international attention for the Munster, and fully embraces his inner artist.

4

JUST
START

1990–1999

Tough Love sucks

I'VE GOT THIS GREAT THEORY about life that I got from my dad: If you want to do something, you just start. When people see that you've started something, they will help you. My theory is that we are all part of a mosaic and when people see you are part of a bigger picture, they will help you. That's how it turned out to be when I started designing for real. Although it didn't always go as smoothly as planned.

As the 1990s started, I was the *man*. I went through a big period between 1986 and 1996 where I had a lot of ideas and there was a lot of energy. I opened stores in New York, San Francisco and Chicago. I even owned a building in New York. The most happening of my stores was the one in Soho—all the trendiest people wanted to work there. We had the best parties in the industry, too, especially the wild ones on the Las Vegas strip. They were epic. People still talk about them today.

As the decade began, the scene was all about grunge, led by bands like Nirvana, Soundgarden and Pearl Jam, who all came out of the Pacific Northwest, just like Fluevog did. Forget Docs: in Seattle, my Angel boots were the quintessential kicks to wear with baggy jeans and flannel shirts. Then as the decade progressed there was hip hop, rap, urban, house, techno and electronic music, all-night raves and mosh pits. Vogs took to the dance floor like nobody's business.

And they were my original designs. When I started designing shoes, I didn't copy anyone. I just came up with an image I thought was cool. I didn't know I could draw. I never knew I could make things with my hands. Just start, I told myself, and I did. I just started working with an idea of what a shoe should look like.

One particular heel was an extreme example of when the art in your head just has to get out. You probably know the one I'm talking about. It was the Munster, that curvy platform shoe with the four-inch baroque heel that kicked our androgynous, unisex footwear tradition to the curb. I designed it in 1988, but it was in 1990 when it really stepped out on the world stage. That year, Lady Miss Kier wore it on the cover of Deee-Lite's debut album, *World Clique*, and a year later, Madonna wore it in the movie *Truth or Dare*. It became as much a part of the 1990s house music and underground DJ scene as Docs were in the 1980s punk scene. In 2018, we re-released it for its thirtieth anniversary in soft suedes and special-edition silver and gold glitter leathers,

1990

After Lady Miss Kier wears her Munsters on the cover of Deee-Lite's debut album, *World Clique*, in 1990, the Fluevog brand catches the world's attention.

John celebrates two decades in business with a catalogue entitled "Twenty Years with John Fluevog" in which he coins the phrase, "Don't delay, Fluevog today," or as it's known to Fluevog acolytes: DDFT.

Dave came up with D.D.F.T. You know what that stands for eh!

I still do that!

and people still love it. Back then, though, I didn't sell a single pair in Vancouver, not a one, but it sold really well in New York. That's the shoe that caught international attention.

Today, I design all our shoes. I sketch every day. I design shoes for both men and women, but I've come to realize that I prefer designing women's shoes. Why not? Women are cuter. Besides, I can have more fun with colours and shapes. To be fair, I still make some extravagant styles for men, and I'm blessed to have a small group of male Fluevogers who rock them on a regular basis. I don't know why more men don't.

By the time I started designing our shoes, I'd already been naming them and putting them into families. Today the biggest family is the Angel, which started, fittingly enough, with a sole.

It must have been 1992, and I remember thinking I didn't know enough about the technical side of making shoes. I was sitting at my desk, head in hands, desperate to stop selling Docs. And there on my desk was a business card I'd picked up at a shoe fair a year earlier, from a French company advertising 100 percent natural latex soles. I faxed a note and the next day they got back

to me. And then we were in business with the first Angel soles, which, as Dave Webber quipped, were guaranteed to "resist alkali, water, acid, fatigue and Satan."

Great, right? Too bad they didn't tell me they could only make ten a day. And they were really expensive. That's because the latex came from a kind of tree that grows in

We are all part of a mosaic and when people see you are part of a bigger picture, they will help you.

Southeast Asia, the hevea tree. They tap it and use the natural milk, which is an emulsion that coagulates when it comes into contact with air. Nowadays, since the natural stuff is so expensive and time-consuming to use, most of our products use eco-friendly synthetic latex.

Anyway, that's the first shoe where I put a slogan on the sole. Now all the Angels have it, and most of the other shoe families have their own messages, too.

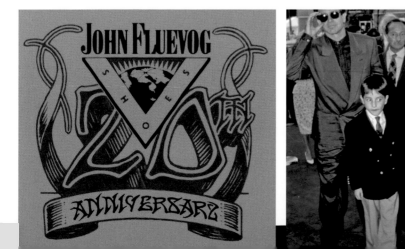

Madonna wears a pair of Munsters to the *Dick Tracy* premiere with Warren Beatty; in 1991, she'd rock the shoes on screen in the movie *Truth or Dare.*

JOHN FLUEVOG SHOES

20TH ANNIVERSARY

The Angel sole's descendants include the Angel shoe, Angel boot, Urban Angel, City Angel, Guardian Angel, Earth Angel, Future Angel, 7th Heaven and so on. Within those families, each shoe has its own name. It could be named for a person I know, or a person I admire; it could be named for a thought, a dream, a thing, a mood, anything that inspires me.

Take James, a member of the Future Angel family. This is a sporty men's shoe named for King James, who spent his childhood reading poetry and grew up to inherit the kingdom of Scotland. His destiny was a dark one, and if he'd only had a pair of Future Angels, they could have protected him from the assassins that eventually took him down. He met his fate when he tried to escape through a sewer, only to find the end had earlier been blocked by his own command. The shoe family comes with a message anyone would be advised to follow: "Your sole will direct your future."

The slogans are just things that come to me. The brand and the shoes are at one level, and the messages take them to another one. It's not just a cute pair of shoes. Sometimes the messages are random and scattered. Sometimes they come from events around me.

Sometimes they're very specific. I have noticed that I need to pay attention to them and write them down. These stories/phrases/ditties form part of the energy and vibe around the shoes and are as important to me as the shoes themselves. They are gifts that I pass along.

My values system, deeper things, space, mysticism are all layered into the brand.

Some messages are pretty clear. The Conquer boot urges you to "pick your battles!" The Choice shoe advises, "To love or to hate, the choice is yours." The Body Parts line, which was all about AIDS awareness and features a heel shaped like a penis, states, "Your body parts are not communal property." More often, the messages are ambiguous, with dual meanings, like the Swordfish, with its pointy toe, which tells you to "stay sharp." Most of all, they are positive, because I believe you should love yourself for who you really are.

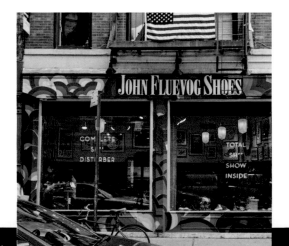

Fluevog Shoes opens in New York's Soho neighbourhood.

Angel soles appear to John in a celestial dream. Or perhaps in the form of a pamphlet from a shoe fair in England. They are the first to carry the message: "Resists alkali, water, acid, fatigue and Satan." They are followed by the Angel shoe, Angel boot, Super Vogs, Racer Boot and Grand National.

No.30-8243: Angelic Sole, Multicolour Ruboff Leather, Men's & Ladies' $179. No.31- Angelic Brogue: Angelic Sole, Multicolour

94   1992   1993

It's no mystery that I hope that my shoes—and their messages—make people dream a little bit and walk in a different world, a world I call Vogville. We all need that from time to time. Life can suck and be difficult. We all need to step out and pretend once in a while.

My values system, deeper things, space, mysticism are all layered into the brand. These are not just shoes; they can take you to a different place. People really got into my shoes, and I believe that's one of the reasons, even though they might not know it. The messages are an important part of the brand to me.

Anyway, up until the mid-1990s, things were going really well for me, at least on the surface. Underneath, of course, I was still the same insecure person, filled with anxiety and self-doubt.

Then, in 1995, my dad died. He was eighty-two and had Alzheimer's disease. It was hard to watch him decline. Sigurd had always been bigger than life, the smartest guy in the room, the guy who could do anything he put his mind to. He introduced me to cars and music and God. I looked up to him, but I often felt I couldn't live up to his expectations. His death knocked me for a loop.

Right around then, other things started to fall apart.

The wholesale side of the business dried up. Cash flow was bad. I had a lot of commitments, and there wasn't much wiggle room financially. I was fifty years old and kind of unravelling. So in 1998, I did what I did at the beginning: I opened another retail store, mainly to keep the volume of production up. But this time, my strategy didn't work out quite as well.

I found myself in Chicago with a vision of a building that would be a beacon for the Midwest. There I came across a rundown old movie theatre in Bucktown, where all the record stores and hip clubs were. It was exactly what I was looking for, exactly what Fluevog fans would be looking for. I had no money but signed the lease anyway and started to put the store together.

Turned out the building had a leaky roof, holes in the floor and no heat, which caused the pipes to freeze and burst in the cold Chicago winter, facts I learned as I started to renovate the store. I was doing as much of the work myself as possible to save money, and despite the cold, I was practically living there, flying back and forth to Vancouver when I could to see my family.

No booze inside this heel !

For Absolut Vodka's 1994 ad campaign, John Fluevog and Ken Rice distilled a metallic leather wedge platform that is always ready to party. Now part of the Bata Shoe Museum collection in Toronto.

Sigurd Fluevog dies after a struggle with Alzheimer's disease, and John buys his dad's Jaguar Mark X from the estate.

Fluevog Shoes opens on San Francisco's Haight Street.

1994   1995   1997

95

On one of those trips home, I discovered that my marriage had fallen apart. Ingrid and I had been together for twenty-one years, all through the days of making clogs with Peter Fox, raising two kids and the challenges of me going out on my own and becoming a designer. I thought we'd be together forever, but that's not what happened. I didn't know what hit me. I really didn't know that emotional pain could hurt so much physically. Now I know.

I was devastated, but I had no choice, I had to carry on and get the store opened. So back I went to Chicago.

It was November. I wasn't eating or sleeping much. One Sunday morning I woke up at 4 a.m. and started walking through the city streets. I passed many different churches as I did, Lutheran, Presbyterian, Catholic. It was getting to be 8:30 or 9 a.m. when I noticed a plastic lit-up sign on which was written in block letters, Primitive Baptist Church.

A Black man was standing outside holding a Bible, and I said to myself, this is it.

I came back later for the service. I walked into a massive sloping auditorium that could have accommodated eight hundred people, although there were only around thirty in the congregation. A Hammond B3 organ started playing the coolest jazz and blues chords. The choir made their way down the aisle, swaying to the music, and began rocking the house. Then the soloist came out and gave it his all. It was awesome and I thought to myself, I'd pay money to hear this.

Although it was a full house on stage, the auditorium remained pretty empty. It felt like the service was all for me, like I had stepped into another dimension and was being given a gift.

Then an elderly Black man shuffled up to the podium. His name was Brother Lincoln and, although he'd clearly had tougher times than trying to open a shoe store, he said a powerful prayer of thanksgiving. He thanked his Creator for waking him up that morning, for helping him to walk to church and for allowing him to stand there on that day. "Amen," choir and congregation called out to him. "Praise Jesus."

After that, the minister got up to speak and she said, "The Lord woke me up at 3 a.m. this morning with a message that I know is for someone out there." Well, there I was, with my dyed blond spiky hair, feeling conspicuously out of place in this African-American

One of my favourites

FLUEVOG

After starting the decade on a high, business takes a dramatic turn for the worse. The wholesale business has dried up. Sales are down. Cash is tight. So John decides to repeat what worked for him in the 1980s and opens a new store, this one in Chicago.

At the end of the year, John's marriage to Ingrid unravels and so does he. In Chicago, he finds himself at Primitive Baptist Church where the minister has a life-changing message for him: "God won't take you to any place that you can't bear," she says.

John sells all his cars except the white Austin Dorset he bought in 1973. He drops his salary to subsistence level. Sells the building in New York. Moves into a basement suite. And then he starts designing the cutest shoes you can imagine. John Fluevog takes the first steps on a whole new path.

church, yet I knew she was speaking directly to me. "You think you have it bad now, you think things can't get no worse," she continued, her voice growing louder. "Well, I'm here to tell you that things *can* get worse!" She was almost shouting now. "But I'm here to tell you that God won't take you to any place that you can't bear." The organ started up in dramatic fashion and a strange and wondrous thing happened. I had a clear vision in my head of an infinitely white place. No walls, no ceiling, only clean white space as far as I could see. A red spiky blob-like thing was lying in the middle of it. I understood that the blob was my broken heart and the spiky things were the shattered pieces of my life. And I knew that where it was broken, the healing spirit could get in and reach all the places it never could before.

I left the church in a daze and went back to the store to continue working. Around 6 p.m., I locked up and was walking up Milwaukee Avenue, thinking of Brother Lincoln and gratitude, when suddenly an intense light flashed on the right side of my brain. It so overwhelmed me, I could barely stand. I started to weep uncontrollably. I staggered to a back alley littered with old mattresses and junk. I leaned up against a chain-link fence and wept for what seemed like an hour. And there, in that dangerous alley right where the L train from O'Hare Airport went underground, I was cleansed and healed.

I have never forgotten that experience.

Later, it did get worse, but as the minister promised, God never did take me to any place that I could not bear.

The Chicago store opened in 1999. My second marriage ended, and business continued to be difficult. I had to sell all my cars except the white Austin Dorset I'd had since 1973. I sold the building in New York. I dropped my salary to subsistence level, and moved out of my home and away from my kids. All my foundations were gone.

As the 1990s started, I had everything. Love. Family. A successful business. Fame. Even an artistic outlet. As the decade ended, I'd lost almost everything. But I knew now that "God won't take you to any place that you can't bear."

I could bear it. I'd have to, right? Once again, I'd just have to start.

And that would be the beginning of the resurrection of John Fluevog. JF

I seemed to like dressing up! weird?

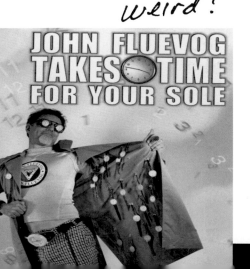

The late actor Robin Williams was a frequent visitor to the store and wore Fluevogs for years.

1999

HOW A SHOE BECOMES A SHOE

From John's brain to your foot.

There's a saying in shoemaking: The last comes first. But that's not quite true. Before you get to the last— the form around which a shoe is made— you have to have the idea and the inspiration. In fact, there are easily more than one hundred steps in designing and making a pair of shoes, from drafting the pattern to hand-cutting the leather, dyeing and finishing the materials, closing and lasting the uppers, and applying the soles and heels. Here's how we make John Fluevog Shoes.

PREVIOUS PAGE Every shoe begins with a sketch, and John sketches shoes every day.

The Inspiration

1

I used to do everything myself, from sketching the shoes to choosing the fabrics to making the moulds and even some of the parts by hand. My team will tell you that I was too involved in making the shoes. But now I've handed over most of the day-to-day tasks and focus on the design. I just keep drawing and my team makes it happen. I travel the world and ideas come to me. And then I start sketching. I sketch a shoe every day. Sometimes I sketch more than one. I capture myths, messages, snippets of inspiration that express the mood, the vibe of the season. My team calls me the "Mystic Traveller." I think I like that.

2

The Design

Once I have a sketch that I think would make a good shoe, I post it on our internal blog and then the design team, led by Arabella Barros, weighs in. Arabella gets what I'm trying to do. Arabella comes from Brazil, which has

one of the world's biggest and best footwear-manufacturing industries. She has worked with me since 2011; in 2014 she became head of women's design and in 2017 became head of the whole design department. I trust her to make the shoe a reality. Of course, not every shoe makes the cut. Arabella says she has a "ten days" rule: If I don't revisit a shoe within ten days of posting it, she figures it's not that important to me. But if it is important, the team drops everything to make it happen. I think she might know me better than I know myself.

ST. JOHN THE BAPTIST PARISH LIBRARY
2920 NEW HIGHWAY 51
LAPLACE, LOUISIANA 70068

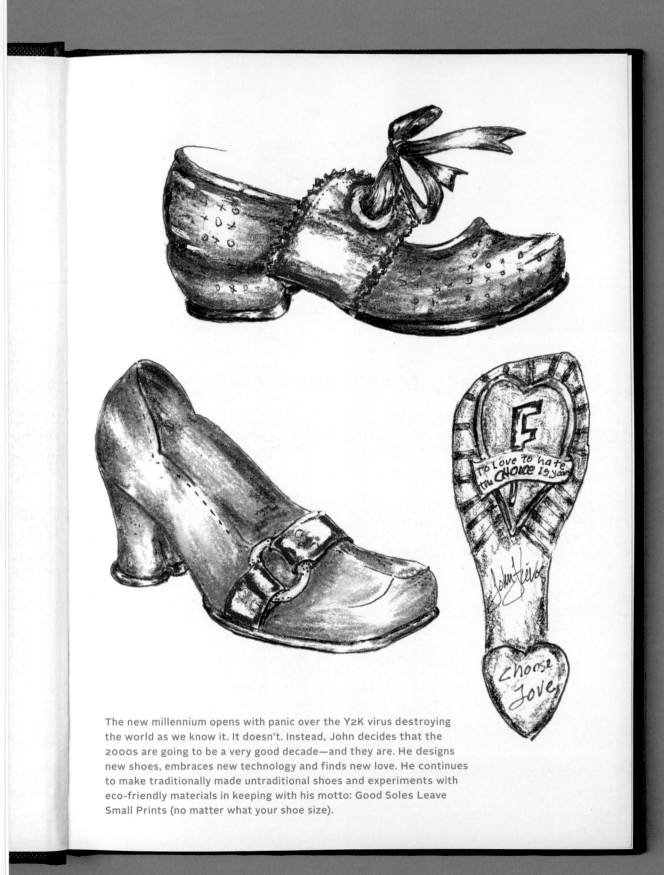

The new millennium opens with panic over the Y2K virus destroying the world as we know it. It doesn't. Instead, John decides that the 2000s are going to be a very good decade—and they are. He designs new shoes, embraces new technology and finds new love. He continues to make traditionally made untraditional shoes and experiments with eco-friendly materials in keeping with his motto: Good Soles Leave Small Prints (no matter what your shoe size).

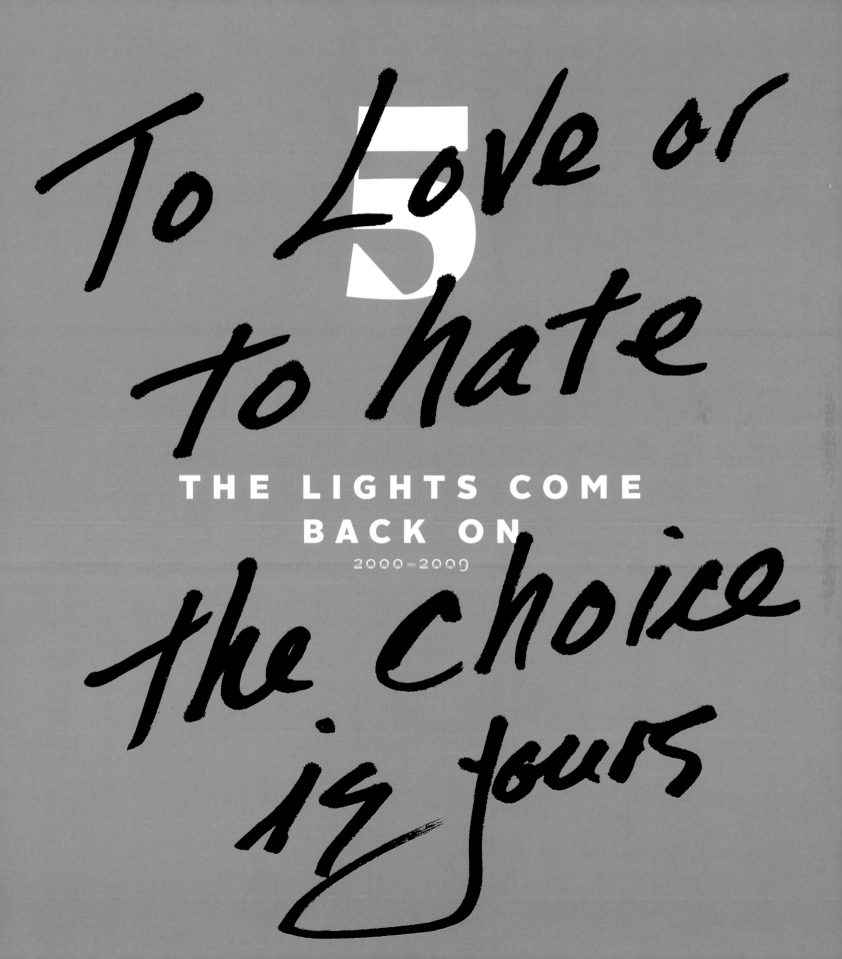

To Love or
to hate

5

**THE LIGHTS COME
BACK ON**
2000–2009

the choice
is yours

AT THE END OF THE 1990S, after opening the Chicago store and my wife leaving, I basically sat at my desk for a year and cried. I'd lost all my cash assets and was practically bankrupt. I was living in a gloomy basement apartment. It was dark. It was bleak. But there was something weirdly attractive about it. It was a struggle, but it was cool. It was rock 'n' roll. It was grit. It was also the foundation of everything that was to come. I realize now that I had to give everything up so I could build everything back up again. I call this chapter of my life "The Remaking of John" or "The Lights Come Back On."

The first step was to focus on the shoes. From bits and pieces, I produced a funky little shoe called the Mini. That was the time of *Sex and the City* and all those brutally uncomfortable shoes with their pointy toes and high heels. I'd sold those stiletto-heeled shoes in the 1980s and I was like, no way, I'm not going to do that again.

Instead, I made these cutie-pie round-toed Mary Janes with a sturdy rubber F-sole and a low, chunky heel. They were the anti-stiletto. They were as comfortable as they were cute and I was convinced they would sell. I was right: Those shoes were the rebirth of the company. They became iconic with Fluevog, and we're still selling versions of them today, with names like Gorgeous and Babycake.

It really surprises me sometimes what sells well. It's more of a wild card than you'd think. But if it wasn't so challenging, I'd probably get bored and do something else.

It's a funny thing. People think that fashion is all about glamour. In fact, the business I'm in is all about numbers. It's all about inventory and crunching numbers, getting inventory in and selling it in quantities that guarantee you can do it again in three months or six months. It's a mathematical quagmire. And then you mix it together with this concept of things that look good and feel good. You need two sides of the brain to be successful in this business. If you're just about the art, you're not going to make it. To do that as the company has expanded, I've had to hire an army of people, and I've had to pull a part of my brain off and give it over to them. It's hard. I never believe anyone else can do a job as well as I can, until I see them doing it better.

Mini Lily

▲▲▲▲▲▲▲▲▲▲▲▲▲▲▲▲▲▲▲▲▲▲▲▲▲▲▲

Do not be fooled by images of sex as beauty.

2000

After opening the Chicago store in 1999, John sits at his desk for a year and cries. But in 2000, "the lights come back on." He designs a "cutie-pie" shoe called the Mini, makes it in six or seven colours, and it's an instant success.

He starts selling shoes online.

And he meets Ruth Stec.

When you're running a smaller company like ours, everything is more personal. I've been working with some of my team for thirty years. By and large I'm friends with everyone who's ever worked here. I'm proud of that. Proud? *Thankful* would be a better word. It's like family.

Business is not business. It's about people working together for a common goal. When you're expanding, that's an important thing to keep in mind. There are very few independent boutiques left that do their own designs. There's a reason for that. It's hard. It's relentless. It's always fight or flight. You cannot rest. You always have to put out another season.

Anyway, around 2000 I decided that I would put together fashion stuff that works well, that you could wear at work all day and then out for fun at night. It would look as good at the end of the year. It would last.

When I started to design my own shoes I just happened to dovetail with the culture of the time. But by 2002, I'd realized that connecting to current culture was grasping at something I couldn't hold on to because cultural moments always move on. And that's when I became independent in my approach, both in

terms of the types of shoes I designed, and how I would sell them.

For one thing, I got serious about selling shoes on the Internet. Online shopping had only started to become a thing in the mid-1990s; eBay and Amazon both launched in 1995. Back then, conventional wisdom was that shoes and pets were going to be the two things that were not sellable online. I proved them wrong (at least when it came to shoes—not pets).

I really wondered who... or why anyone would buy shoes on line...but they did.

In 2000, I became one of the first people to sell shoes online, and right away our shoes started selling. The website is still one of the biggest sales sources for the company. Retailing has changed a lot because of the Internet, and we've benefited from it a lot.

She's as nice as she looks!

John and Ruth marry in a surprise ceremony at the Granville Street store.

John launches Open Source Footwear to turn shoe wearers into shoe designers. They submit designs and John turns his favourites into real-life shoes.

John introduces the Future Angel, Rodeo Star and Choice families of footwear.

That said, I'm still a big believer in brick-and-mortar stores. It's important and, for us, it's necessary. Maybe that's because the Fluevog brand is tough to understand from a picture. You need to connect with the people who are part of it.

Still too cash-strapped to open any new stores, in 2002 I also launched Open Source Footwear. Taking a page from open-source software—the concept of making computer program design publicly accessible so people can modify and share it—Open Source Footwear gave everyone a chance to have a say in the shoes they wanted to see, and it's still something we do from time to time. We asked people to submit their designs and if your design inspired me, I'd make it into a shoe, name it for you, add it to the collection and send you a pair. Pretty neat, right?

For instance, there was the shoe designed by Jody Elizabeth from Ohio, which was inspired by the ball-and-claw feet and cabriole legs on antique, Chippendale-style furniture—we made it into a high-heeled Mary Jane and called it the Queen Transcendent Elizabeth. The Nanette equestrian boot was inspired (and named) by Janet Erwin of North Carolina. The Love Rodeo

Watson was a sporty loafer DJ Watson of Coventry, UK, designed for his girlfriend.

In addition to Open Source Footwear, we also invited Fluevogers to vote on their favourite colourways for the next season's new styles. We called it VogPopuli. ("Yes, Fluevogers, you are part of history. This is where Fluevogers from all over the galaxy convene to make their voices heard—and heard, you will be.")

Our customers have been some of our best collaborators.

I believe in the philosophy that brands in general belong as much to the people who use them as the people who own them. It really is important when it comes to building community, and community is at the heart of who we are. It's very personal, a brand connection. And this one is really something.

Social media and the Internet have been great tools for us. I believe in paying attention, in learning about

Fluevog Shoes opens in Los Angeles.

John designs the Blackspot sneaker for Kalle Lasn of Adbusters: it's pro-environment, anti-sweatshop and super successful. Years later, Lasn kicks off the Occupy Wall Street protest movement.

Black Spot Sneaker V2.0

new things that are connected, and I've found that the Internet is a wonderful way to connect people and ideas. Just think about it. If you're interested in, say, underwater trombone solos, before the Internet, you would have had a hard time finding anyone who shared your interest. But now it's easy to connect with them with just a few keystrokes. Of course it has its dark side. I'm not really an end-of-the-world kind of guy, but I can see the world is changing so quickly it makes society feel insecure and wonder what's happening next.

Our customers have been some of our best collaborators, but we've also worked with other artists to come up with cool designs. In 2005, for instance, I collaborated with singer-songwriter Courtney Taylor-Taylor of The Dandy Warhols, an alternative band from Portland, and we designed a sleek boot that excited music and fashion lovers alike. In 2011, I worked with l.a. Eyeworks to create a limited-edition pair of sunglasses called VogVision. And, since my idea of Flying Vogs never actually took off, in 2013, I worked with Air Canada Rouge to get my shoes in the air via the feet of their in-flight staff. Recently, I've collaborated on collections with labels including the cutting edge luxury label

Comme des Garçons, New York's Opening Ceremony, and my friend Anna Sui.

Back in the early 2000s, though, it took a little while for things to get better. Business eventually picked up. The Mini was a hit. I introduced more shoes. The Rodeo Star. Choice. Future Angels. In 2004, I opened a store in Los Angeles, the first new store since Chicago in 1999. The light was coming through the darkness. And I met Ruth Stec. I met her at church, not all that long after Ingrid and I separated. Ruth is tall and striking and beautiful. People, when they meet her, they're about her. She's so lovely. She is magnetic. She allows me to be who I am. She's cool with herself. She has a strong identity and it doesn't diminish her to help others. She doesn't wrap her success around me. She travels with me everywhere, and I don't think I'd like to travel without her. She wants to grow old with somebody, and that somebody is me.

I married her in 2002, in the Granville Street store, on her birthday. It was a surprise wedding. We invited people to come celebrate her birthday, and gave them a surprise wedding instead.

And then we were living in marital bliss. It was quite lovely. We lived in her apartment, which was in a modest

Let's really be Thankful!

John Fluevog collaborates with Courtney Taylor-Taylor of The Dandy Warhols on a boot.

three-storey walk-up in Vancouver's West End. Business began to pick up. I started to learn I couldn't do everything myself, that I had to let marketing and accounting do their thing. It opened things up for the company to grow. I opened another store, in Montreal, and it worked.

Things were looking really bright—and then suddenly they weren't. It seemed like the same dance all over again.

In 2007 the lease on the Granville Street store was coming up for renewal. I'd had that lease since the late 1980s, and even though it was a small space, it was my flagship store and my head office, where I did all my accounting and my designs and everything. More importantly, it was the constant. To lose it would be like losing a part of myself. But I was having a hard time connecting with the landlord, and suddenly I found myself looking for a new space just as real estate prices were skyrocketing.

Then I heard that something was going on at the Richard Kidd store in Gastown. For years the space had been a parking lot between two old brick buildings, but in the early 2000s, it was transformed into a two-level glass-and-steel infill with forty-two-foot glass ceilings

and exposed brick walls. In 2004, this ultra-hip luxury lifestyle boutique called Richard Kidd opened in the space. (Rich kid—get it?) Now rumour had it that it might be coming up for lease.

So I hired an agent, who called the landlord, and they negotiated to let the Richard Kidd people out of their lease. Great. Then, as luck would have it, right after that I ran into my Granville Street landlord and his wife. I started talking with her and said, "Your husband won't talk to me." A few hours later, my cellphone jingled in my pocket. It was the landlord. He said, "Maybe we can work something out." And that's how in 2008 I ended up with two locations in Vancouver.

That was really the moment when everything changed. It was the first time in more than twenty years that I had two stores in one city—two stores in *my* city—and it triggered a lot of anxiety. It felt like the early 1980s all over again, when I had to close everything and I was on the verge of bankruptcy. I felt insecure about opening something so grand and paying two really expensive leases. I was concerned we were going to fail, that we would never have enough customers to support such a palatial store.

This store was featured on an episode of a home & garden T.V. show. I thought it might be my big T.V. break ... It wasn't.

Fluevog Shoes opens in Montreal.

Jack White rocks the Jack boot.

But to my shock, from the day we opened the doors in Gastown, the store was a success. Moving to this location was a turning point for the brand. It was the thing that proved to an insecure kid that people weren't going to say: "Who do you think you are?" We all go through moments when we think we're not good enough, we're not enough, and that was mine. Then I realized that if I could do this, I could open more stores. So I did. And every store worked!

Opening the Gastown store opened up my horizons. If I hadn't gone through that soul-searching and terrorizing experience, I would never have opened up two stores in the same city. Now I have two stores in San Francisco because I found out I could do it in Vancouver. And I have two stores in Boston, two stores in Toronto, two stores in Montreal and two stores in New York, along with single stores in fourteen other cities.

It was like somebody was saying to me—because I wasn't listening—"Hey, Fluevog, you can do it. You can do two stores." Through the adversity, through the difficulty, came something quite wonderful.

Now, for perhaps the first time in my life, everything was on a solid footing. My home life was blissful.

Business was good, and getting better. My creativity had taken flight. I no longer felt I wasn't good enough. And I felt whole and at home in my faith.

For me, business has a global emotional connection; my spirituality is a sense of personal transcendence. I always had a desire to go into the spiritual side of my life. It's the place where I've always felt the most comfortable and at peace with myself. The most whole. It's a contemplative place.

We all go through moments when we think we're not good enough, and that was mine.

If I could, I would encourage people to step out and do things that are beyond what they think they can do. Step out in faith. Just put your foot out—you may not know what's happening, but trust in faith and you will end up on solid ground. JF

The design team works up stairs

Fluevog Shoes opens again in Vancouver's Gastown, the first time John has had two stores in one city since the 1980s. This is a huge turning point for the brand. John introduces the Radio family of shoes: "Tune in, turn on, and Vog out!"

After two years of work, John finishes restoring his dad's Jaguar Mark X, now renamed "The Fluevog."

FluevogCreative, a platform that brings advertising back to the people, launches and thrusts Fluevog into the future. By the end of the decade, John slowly starts handing creative control to his team.

CULT/URE

Meet the independent, quirky, dynamic, dramatic, stylish, comfortable, sometimes weird but always well-shod people who love John Fluevog Shoes. (John loves them right back.)

"Suddenly, there they were: the Munsters, shiny and glittering. I snatched the last pair right up, even though they were a size too big!"

LADY MISS KIER, DJ, FASHION ICON, VOCALIST, DEEE-LITE

It takes a certain amount of confidence to kick it in a shoe that is a little out of step with trends. Maybe only one or two people in a hundred like our shoes, but those people like them a lot. And once someone is a fan, they're a fan for life. They're also part of a community that has its own language and traditions. Fluevogers come from all walks of life. I have a lot of brainiac customers, artistic customers and customers who work on their feet all day. But don't listen to me. Listen to what Fluevogers have to say for themselves.

PREVIOUS PAGE Lady Miss Kier became the first celebrity Fluevoger when she wore the Munster on the cover of Deee-Lite's *World Clique.*

A glimpse inside the Vog Vault in the Toronto store on Queen Street

Legendary drag queen Sasha Velour is a fan of the Munster, considering it as much a work of art as article of clothing.

"The original Munster shoe might be one of the best pieces of design I have ever seen. I have a stunning silver glitter pair and while they are a dream to wear, I choose to keep them on my mantel alongside other works of art. Looking at them brings me such joy!"

SASHA VELOUR, AMERICAN DRAG LEGEND

CHERRY VELVETY

In my Fluevogs, I'm rediscovering who I am after motherhood took over my entire identity.

PRINCESS
NDIP, QC, CANADA

Fluevog is my daily anchor, confidence-giving machine and self-proclaimer!

JULIE
DENVILLE, NJ, USA

Not only do they make my heart smile, they are my shield of confidence especially when I am feeling blue.

SUE
WELLINGTON, NZ

MISS KATWISE

> It was 1993 when I went off to Alaska to sling salmon on a processing ship. Upon my return to Seattle my new badass friend introduced me to Fluevog. Wow, what a store! What amazing shoes!! Holy cow, my life changed forever!!! Boring shoes be gone!

DEB
BILLINGS, MT, USA

———

Many years ago, a girl I madly crushed on wore a pair of burgundy Derby Swirls. While my crush on her faded, I never lost my love for those boots. I bought my own pair and whenever I wore them, I felt like I was walking on clouds. I was resistant to alkali, water, acid, fatigue and Satan. I was badass.

SUZANNE
MONTREAL, QC, CANADA

———

My Fluevogs represent milestones in my life. Met my husband. Got that promotion. All while wearing a pair of Fluevogs. Each pair has a sentimental memory and makes me walk a little taller with pride and love.

DANA
KELOWNA, BC, CANADA

———

In 1987 I went to the Fluevog store in Vancouver because I heard from somebody in Portland that this was a place you could get vampire shoes. We needed vampire shoes. We arrived dressed in black and all we wanted to do was hang out in the store all day, hoping and thinking we were cool. I still have my first pair of Fluevogs.

RENEE
VANCOUVER, BC, CANADA

This is a decade of fast and furious growth for Fluevog Shoes. At last, it seems, the world is ready to accept the doctrine of Fluevog. John opens nineteen stores, including his first overseas, puts his efforts into charity and receives the kind of recognition he could once only dream of. Still, life has surprises in store, and they're not always the good kind. As the decade ends, John Fluevog prepares to celebrate fifty years of resisting the ordinary.

6

Exceed

your own

STEPPING

OUT

2010—2019

expectations

TWO THOUSAND AND TEN. That February, the world came to Vancouver. The XXI Olympic and Para-lympic Winter Games saw more than three thousand athletes from eighty-two nations compete in and around Vancouver. Thousands and thousands of visitors came to cheer them on. They say 1.8 billion people watched on TV. I guess they liked what they saw because that was the year Canada became the world's top tourism destination. It was wild.

Here in Gastown, people would come into the store speaking every language under the sun. There was so much energy in the city, you could feel it vibrating. It was a powerful moment, seeing what could happen when all that energy comes together. And it dawned on me that it's something we've been doing, as a company, for decades, even though it wasn't something I set out to do.

The thing is, my shoes, they're not just a product. They're a culture. A message. An idea. They tell people, it's OK to be different. Not just OK—beautiful. I remember when our chief marketing officer, Stephen Bailey, launched the "No, *you're* weird" campaign in 2010. We've always been different, but somehow that season our styles must have been really different from whatever the trends were. I remember we had wholesale accounts that just couldn't get on board. But instead of worrying

about it, we decided to celebrate it. Being weird was just part of who we were. Our staff was weird. Our customers were weird. We might not be for you. We're a different breed. We're weird. And actually...so are you. So why don't we all embrace it and celebrate it?

Those three words sound so simple now, but Stephen had been wrestling with the idea for about six months before it came together. Once it did, we put a big sign in the window saying, "No, *you're* weird." People would come in, laughing. They'd been standing outside thinking, "Those shoes are so weird." And then they'd catch sight of the sign and go, oh. We even had a contest, asking customers to embrace their weirdness and send us a photo of themselves at their weirdest for a chance to win $1,000 in shoe dollars. People got weird.

It's incredibly meaningful to refuse to follow what everyone else is doing. That's the feedback we got from the people who walked into the store, people from Russia and China and Europe and South America. They loved our shoes and what they were about. It was, perhaps, the first time I realized that I was, at last, a business success. I wish my father had been around to see it.

So it might seem counterintuitive that it was then that I decided to start stepping back from the business. Just a little bit, though—I would focus on the design and let the inspiration take me where it wanted to. But the

2010

The XXI Olympic Winter Games bring the world to Vancouver, and most of it wanders through John's stores.

Fluevog Shoes opens in San Francisco's Union Square.

John and Nooka team up to design a watch.

Fast Company ranks John Fluevog Shoes one of the Most Innovative Companies in the Fashion Industry.

To celebrate the fortieth anniversary of Fluevog Shoes, the Museum of Vancouver opens the exhibit "Fox, Fluevog & Friends."

The FlueMarket is created to allow Fluevogers to sell/swap/find their favourite Vogs.

John and l.a. Eyeworks create the VogVision, a limited-edition pair of sunglasses.

In June, as the Stanley Cup riots rage in downtown Vancouver, John is in hospital, diagnosed with leukemia. He comes close to dying, but angels are on hand to heal his body and faith. Six months later, he's back at work.

day-to-day stuff, making the shoes, going to the trade shows, worrying about marketing and accounting and all that, I would let someone else handle. It wasn't easy, letting go, but I gradually handed the reins to my son Adrian, who is now the CEO, and let the team do the work of sourcing the material, producing the shoes and continuing to build this community and culture.

The hardest part was letting go of some of the design elements. I'd done everything myself for so long, it was really difficult handing things over to my design team, especially since I still wanted to have a say in everything that was happening. Getting them to work as a unit was, as one of them said, a bit "like getting cats in a bag to work together." I wanted each of them to contribute their unique energies to our designs, but it seemed that the more freedom I gave the team, the more dysfunctional it became.

Something was fundamentally wrong and I didn't know how to fix it.

While this was going on, Ruth and I attended the Quebec City jazz fest, where we heard a contemplative jazz duo, two musicians working together, one on piano and one on guitar, weaving seamlessly in and out of the music, following no score or apparent melody. At the break, we spoke to them. "You probably think there is no leader, that we are following each other depending on who comes up with the next chord," one of them said to me. Well, yes. Not so, he added. There actually is a leader. One of them hears the music in his mind and begins playing it. The other follows.

It hit me in a moment of crystal clarity that this was what was wrong with my design team. Some were playing jazz, some rock 'n' roll, some disco and some classical. I was not laying down the vibe. I was not giving them the overall theme. I was looking for them to give it to me. In fact, it was me as a leader that was the problem and not them.

This revelation changed my leadership style and I became a stronger, bolder, more forthright leader as a result. The team is now happier and functions so much better than it did before. Most importantly, each player now knows what style of shoe "music" is being played and can add their own flourish to it.

Handing responsibility to the team turned out to be the best thing I could have done. Now my business is doing well and I have never had so little to do with it. Between 2010 and 2018, we opened nineteen more stores across North America and our first overseas location in Amsterdam in March 2018.

It started with San Francisco. On September 16, 2010, we opened our second store in the City by the Bay, this one in Union Square. It was a leap of faith—especially

We're far from Perfect but We've come a long WAy!

NO, YOU'RE WEIRD!

The first permanent Flueseum opens upstairs at the Calgary store.

Two Ten Footwear Foundation names John Fluevog as Shoe Person of the Year.

Fluevog Shoes opens in Minneapolis and Washington, DC.

John teams up with Air Canada Rouge to design shoes for their flight attendants.

Fluevog Shoes opens in Portland, Calgary, Quebec City, Denver, and a second store in Toronto, in the Distillery District.

since without investors we were totally dependent on sales—but the success of our second store in Vancouver assured me that it would work. And it did.

Less than a year later, on April 19, 2011, we opened a store in Portland, followed by one in Quebec City on June 1 and one in Calgary on July 5. In 2012, we opened stores in Washington, DC, and Minneapolis. In 2013 came our Denver store and a second Toronto store (the Distillery) followed, then Ottawa in 2014. In 2015, we opened two stores, one on Abbot Kinney Boulevard in Venice, California, and another in New Orleans. That same year we moved our Queen Street store in Toronto down the street to a bigger location. We were even busier in 2017, opening four locations: a second store in Montreal (Vieux-Port) and our first stores in Edmonton, Victoria and Brooklyn. Then in 2018, we opened the Amsterdam store and a second store in Boston (Faneuil Hall), and shifted the one on Newbury down the street to a larger location.

Each one was its own adventure, but Amsterdam was something special, and not just because it was our first store in Europe. We'd been considering Europe for a long time—we'd been eyeing Berlin and Stockholm as well, and I'd contemplated opening a store in London since I began. But somehow it had never been quite right, until Amsterdam.

The city had always been on our list. There's a real connection between the Dutch and Canadians. There's a similarity between us, a strong but subtle confidence, a sly sense of humour, a quiet hospitality and a playfulness in fashion. Their style tends to be conservative, except when it comes to shoes and accessories, where they're allowed some room to play. That was a perfect fit for Fluevog.

And we just loved the space itself. It was the only one we looked at that amazed us right away. Don't forget, with opening stores, we have to design in two realms: shoes and the stores themselves. Even though all our stores look different, there's a similarity of spirit to them. In part that's because there isn't the budget to build everything from scratch. When there isn't a budget to make it look amazing, it already has to be amazing in its raw form, so we look for spaces with a certain energy. Part of what gives the stores their unique vibe is the work of Chapel Arts. They're a Vancouver company; you could almost call them a collective, just like our clog makers in the 1970s, only these guys aren't working with leather, but with wood and metal. They're the ones responsible for the live-edge tables you see in several of our recent stores.

We also introduced hundreds of new shoes this decade, including instant classics like the Cubist Cupcake,

John Fluevog creates his own Fluevogian language inscribed as secret messages on some of his footwear.

Fluevog Shoes opens in Ottawa.

John's cancer returns, and once again, he fights it off.

Fluevog Shoes opens its Abbot Kinney Boulevard store, in Venice, California.

John opens a Fluevog pop-up shop on Facebook's campus in Menlo Park, California.

John collaborates with local breweries across North America to throw a series of 45 Years of Cheers parties at participating Fluevog stores, featuring limited-edition custom growlers and original artwork prints.

In Toronto, the Queen Street store moves down the street into a former TD Bank building, now transformed into a beautiful boutique complete with patio and the world's one and only gravity-defying Vog Vault.

Fluevog Shoes opens in New Orleans's French Quarter, the first store in the South.

John celebrates forty-five years in the shoe business by releasing a limited-edition shoe on Fluevog Day. It is aptly named The 45.

an ankle boot variation on the Swordfish that Lady Gaga made famous on a walk through New York, and the Seraphina boot, which Beyoncé wore in her "Formation" music video. (They're not the only celebs who love Fluevog shoes, of course: Alice Cooper has rocked the Swordfish styles for decades, and Jack White kicked it with the Jack boot on stage for more than ten years.)

And finally, throughout the decade, I was getting the kind of recognition that made my insecurities (mostly) a thing of the past.

In 2010, I was honoured with a forty-year retrospective exhibit at the Museum of Vancouver. They called it "Fox, Fluevog & Friends: The Story behind the Shoes" and hundreds of friends and customers, old and new, came out to say hello at the opening party, most of them wearing their favourite Vogs. Thousands more checked out the exhibit during its two-month run. That same year, *Fast Company* recognized us as one of the Most Innovative Companies in the Fashion Industry, thereby proving that it's possible to celebrate the beauty of the past with excitement for the future. Then, in 2012, I was named Shoe Person of the Year by the Two Ten Footwear Foundation, which provides emergency financial, emotional and educational services to America's 330,000 footwear employees and their families.

We were also building more of a presence online: In 2011, we launched the FlueMarket, which allows people to list, buy, sell and swap Fluevogs for free, right on our site. And in 2014, we relaunched the website itself. The business has moved from one that was hands-on hammer and nails to one that is also technology driven. And as we've grown, and opened more stores and increased our sales, it's allowed me to reconnect with my inner soul.

In 2015, I celebrated forty-five years in the shoe business and, rather than having a nervous breakdown, released a limited-edition shoe on International Fluevog Day (May 15, when we celebrate Random Acts of Fluevog by sharing stories of kindness to help spread love and positivity all throughout the Fluniverse). It featured the iconic vintage Munster heel and was aptly named The 45. We also collaborated with local breweries across North America to throw a series of 45 Years of Cheers parties featuring limited-edition custom growlers and original artwork prints. All guests, drinks and shoes were handled responsibly.

Meanwhile, my personal life couldn't have been better. Ruth and I bought an apartment close to the Gastown store and stepped up our charitable endeavours. We found a getaway on BC's Sunshine Coast, a place where I can recharge my batteries. My kids were doing great.

F.Y.I. I'm a size 10.5

FYI Beyonce is a size 9!

Beyoncé releases her "Formation" music video in which she wears the Seraphina boots.

John's mother, Ruth, quietly passes away.

The exterior of the New York store at the corner of Prince and Mulberry gets a complete makeover courtesy of a beautiful floral mural by artist Jet Martinez.

Lady Gaga takes a stroll through New York in a pair of Cubist Cupcakes.

In 2017, Adrian became the company CEO. Britta has become an artist who weaves social justice into her textile and ceramic artworks. Jonathan is a musician, manager, promoter, producer and documentarian. And just imagine—I'm a grandfather now, five times over.

So things were pretty good. But even while all of this was unfolding, as always, life still had one big lesson waiting for me.

Good times, bad times, dark times, light times.

In the spring of 2011, I started feeling tired. At first I thought it was just the stress of the business and opening so many new stores. But finally I took a blood test to see if there was something more serious going on.

I remember sitting up on the deck of my place in Vancouver. The sun was setting and it was magical, the way it can be here on a June night. Ruth was saying to me, "It's a gorgeous evening. We need to enjoy this because we never know what could happen in the next five minutes or five days." And then the phone rang. It was a doctor from the blood lab saying, "Your white blood cell count is very low." He told me not to go out in any crowds in case I caught something, because my immune system wouldn't be able to handle it. Turned out, I had leukemia.

My first thought was, you got the wrong guy. But he didn't.

I remember the first night I was in the hospital, after Ruth went home, feeling so confused and exhausted and alone. I dreaded the darkness. I'd always had my faith and I was surprised that I was so afraid. What was I afraid of? Dying?

I started taking chemo right away and I had an allergic reaction to the drugs they were giving me. I deteriorated rapidly over the next week and came really close to dying. It was a pretty shocking experience. In the end, I was in hospital for over a month, and then it took a lot longer until I was well enough to go back to work.

I was still in hospital on June 15, when the Stanley Cup hockey finals were being held in Vancouver. The Boston Bruins beat the Vancouver Canucks in the final and deciding game, and the city exploded. Rioters burned cars, broke windows, threw Molotov cocktails, looted stores and attacked bystanders.

John's beloved Chicago store gets a major renovation and reopens to reveal a wall of vintage Fluevog ads, movie theatre seating and a shoeshine throne (built by Union Wood Co) fit for a king.

Adrian Fluevog becomes company CEO.

Fluevog Shoes partners with Fogo Island Inn to create a custom limited-edition shoe, a lichen-coloured variation on the Vow lace-up, to support local culture and industry.

The John Fluevog Shoes Emerging Artist Grant launches. It helps new visual artists develop their skills with $10,000 and a pair of Fluevogs to encourage them to stay on their path.

Fluevog Shoes opens in Vieux-Port, Montreal, complete with three pieces of commissioned artwork by Andy Dixon. Stores also open in Victoria, Brooklyn and Edmonton.

I remember looking out the window of my room at Vancouver General Hospital, watching the smoke curling into the sky over downtown, and thinking, they'd better get the shoes out of the window.

Sure enough, the window had been broken, but one of my son Adrian's friends, Andrew, lived downtown and stood guard outside the store, protecting it from the rioters. It was madness. Meanwhile, my daughter, Britta, got on her bike and rode down to the store— they weren't letting cars into downtown, but she was determined to get there. At 3 a.m. she was in there, sweeping up the broken glass, when a glass truck came by; the driver offered to replace the windows then and there.

Andrew and Britta saved the day, and so did the glass truck guy, while I was in hospital. It was like angels were protecting me. I named a shoe for Andrew in gratitude. I'm pretty sure he got a free pair or two.

While I was sick, everyone kicked in. It made me realize that I could let go, that I didn't have to do every-thing, that I could let others do it instead. And people looked out for me. People prayed for me.

One of the strangest things I remember, an ex-employee from Poland was here visiting and called someone he knew in Israel to come and pray for me. His name was Israel. Israel from Israel. Two weeks later he came out to Vancouver. He hung out for two days and prayed for me. I was so weak I could hardly walk across the room. And then he left. I've never heard from him since. I've tried writing and calling and sending emails, but he just disappeared. Like a spirit, I guess.

But it worked. It made me feel loved. Special. It made me feel I was known. I felt loved by my Creator. I felt loved.

Slowly, I recovered. It took me six months to be well enough to go back to work. And then in 2014, I got sick with leukemia again, and healed again. During that time I had a lot of dreams and visions. I was drawing like crazy. I drew some of my favourite shoes during that time. I was very prolific.

Shortly after that, in 2016, my mom passed away. She was ninety-six, which is an inspiring age, and she had a life well lived. I still miss her gentle spirit, though.

For whatever reason, I've been given more days, and I kind of wonder why. I think it's got something to do with the people in my life. Me deciding what's important to me. And what's important is not my business, it's the Fluevog culture and it's my family. It's passing something on to the next generation. It's why I'm writing this book. It's not all about ourselves. It's about the communities we live in, and the love we can share. JF

I love you for reading this far!

In March, Fluevog Shoes opens in Amsterdam. This is the brand's first overseas location. Fluevog Shoes also opens in Faneuil Hall, Boston.

In August, Fluevog hosts the first annual Flummunity Fest in New Orleans. The second is held in September 2019 in Portland, Oregon. (Destination city is voted on by Fluevogers well in advance.)

After all these years, George Clinton still grooves in our boots, just as he did at a June 2019 Parliament Funkadelic concert in New York.

In late 2019, John heads Down Under to open a store in Melbourne, Australia.

2019

SHOES WITH SOUL

It's always been about more than cute footwear at Fluevog Shoes. Here are some of the company's sustainable, ethical and charitable practices.

FLUEVOGS ARE CRAFTED
IN FAMILY RUN FACTORIES

68%
PORTUGAL

15%
PERU

7%
CHINA

5%
MEXICO

3%
VIETNAM

ALL OVER THE WORLD!

0.012%

CHANCE OF RUNNING INTO SOMEONE
WEARING THE EXACT SAME SHOES AS YOU

FLUEVOGERS RECEIVE
AN AVERAGE OF
2.7
COMPLIMENTS PER DAY

49 COMMON
MISSPELLINGS
OF 'FLUEVOG'

0 BORING
SHOES

65 WATER STREET

My business is making and selling shoes. But if I've learned one thing in fifty years, it's that the best way to make your business a success is to invest in your community. I've always done that, even back in the 1970s when I was hiring street kids to make clogs. You don't have to do what we do, but I hope you do something. Engaging in ethical, sustainable and charitable practices makes your staff happy and your customers think well of you. And besides, it's just the right thing to do.

PREVIOUS PAGE The Fluevog Shoes flagship store in Vancouver's Gastown neighbourhood is one of the city's beloved architectural spaces.

SUPPORTIVE

IF YOU'RE NOT CONSCIOUS of sustainability and social issues, you shouldn't be in design. It's that simple. Well, of course it's not really all that simple. It's a lot easier to make things that pollute the planet and exploit workers than it is to make ethical and sustainable ones. It's a lot easier to make money that way, too. But it's never been what Fluevog Shoes has been about.

There are so many things to give to, and you can't give to everyone. You have to choose which ones to support. We're interested first and foremost in things that affect women and children. If you help children, you invest in our future. If you invest in women, well, they do everything. They usually raise the kids, and they're the ones who take care of the day to day in general. We also are big supporters of the arts—film, theatre, music, visual art—and you'll see Fluevog shoes on stage at Carousel Theatre for Young People in Vancouver, or at Bard on the Beach, just for a couple of examples. At the Gastown store, we do maybe two charity events a month. The staff likes working for a company that does these sorts of things. It's a great idea, right? I mean, why not?

One of our very favourite causes is Saint James Music Academy, which teaches classical music to hundreds of at-risk kids. Gastown, where our store is located, is charming and touristy, but it's also on the edge of the Downtown Eastside, which is one of the poorest neighbourhoods in Canada and has a lot of social problems. Ruth and I work closely with the academy now, but our relationship started a few years back when we held a shoe party in our Gastown store and raised money for the academy. It was win-win-win.

SUSTAINABLE

EVEN BACK IN THE 1980s, when it was all about making money at any cost and no one was even recycling yet, I started introducing sustainable practices throughout the company. I was even crowned King John the Biodegradable in one of our catalogues.

I remember how excited I was to find a natural latex to make my Angel soles, the ones that resist alkali, water, acid, fatigue and Satan. Who needs to dump more pollution into the water and the air, right? And who needs to create more garbage from things you wear only a few times, then throw out? That's why we designed our shoes to make them last. They don't follow trends that last ten minutes. Many of the styles are resoleable. They are made of high-quality leathers that look better over time, not worse. We want you to wear your Vogs for years and years. They are the opposite of fast fashion.

And if you're tired of them, we want you to give them another chance at life by selling them on the FlueMarket. It may seem counterintuitive, but we're thrilled that such a thing exists. The FlueMarket is an online community where Fluevogers can buy, sell and trade their used Vogs. We host it for free on our site and encourage people to shop there. Fluevogers can post their listings from online commerce sites like eBay or Craigslist, or just list their items au naturel. Browse through and you might find that pair of size 9½ Minis you've been craving. Or if you will just die without a pair of size 8 Supervogs in blue and grey, you can post your desire in the Wanted section. Maybe your unicorn is lurking in some other Fluevoger's closet.

It may not be good for the bottom line, but it's the right thing to do. Plus it's a lot of fun, and people love it—the FlueMarket has sold over ten thousand pairs of gently loved Fluevogs.

What else? Early on we introduced some vegan versions of our Angels, which we're bringing back along with some other vegan styles in fall 2019. In 2004, we collaborated with the guys at Adbusters—the Vancouver-based pro-environment media organization founded in 1989 by Kalle Lasn and Bill Schmalz—on a vegan shoe called the Blackspot sneaker, though Adbusters hailed it as the "Unswoosher." Anyway, we did the designs and connected Kalle with the factories. Adbusters sold tens of thousands of shoes. (We don't make any money from them, which is fine.) Boy, that was an experience working with Kalle. He went on to create the Occupy Wall Street protest movement. Talk about connecting with culture.

And right from the early days we insisted on reducing waste and reusing materials when possible—for instance, we use scrap leather as coasters, mouse pads and coin purses in many of our stores.

CHARITABLE

ONE PROJECT WE WORKED ON was with Fogo Island Inn. Fogo is this beautiful, wild, windswept island off the northeast coast of Newfoundland. Its main revenue comes from fishing, which means that it's been through some pretty tough times over the years. The hotel is an incredible work of contemporary architecture that's inspired by the traditional fishermen's houses on the island. More than that, though, it has a mission to contribute to its community in every way, from serving local produce in the restaurant to decorating the guest rooms with furniture and quilts made by local artisans.

In 2017, we collaborated with the inn on a limited-edition Fogo Island shoe to raise money for the Shorefast Foundation, a registered Canadian charity that builds cultural and economic resilience on Fogo Island. The shoe, a cute round-toed lace-up with a medium heel, features the colours of the lichen on the island's rocky shores— purple, orange, brown, pink, blue— and has a special stamped sole.

Fully half the retail sales of the $339 shoe went to Shorefast. Not only that, but the shoe was made in Portugal, which has been a fishing trading partner to Fogo Island. I thought that was pretty cool.

That's only one of many, many charity initiatives we've been involved in over the years. I don't generally like to talk about it too much. It's tooting your own horn, which feels a little gross. But lately I've been thinking that it's important to tell these stories so they might inspire other brands to do the same thing, and they let our staff and customers know what else their shoes are a part of.

My wife, Ruth, oversees most of the charity work we do. Most of it is at the store level, especially at our Canadian stores, and is often something that is close to home in the market. Mostly, though, the staff at each store comes up with their own ideas, runs them past me and Ruth, and then takes it from there. We're also working on catching up and confirming that our real-life staff

teams give a pair of socks to the homeless for every pair of socks we sell.

You know, at the end of the day, you do all this business and you work like a madman and on certain days you get fed up with life. But when you invest in something like this, you can go: At least I did this. I made a difference.

We didn't set out to become a force for raising money and awareness. It just sort of happened. And as it evolved, I saw what a good business move it was. If there was one piece of advice I'd want to pass on to other brands, this is the one thing I'd want to share: Invest in your community. Support those in need. You don't have to follow our model. There are plenty of ways to give back and there are plenty of causes that need help and support. Helping them makes you feel good. And it's good for business, too.

More than anything, for a brand, you want people to think well when they think of you.

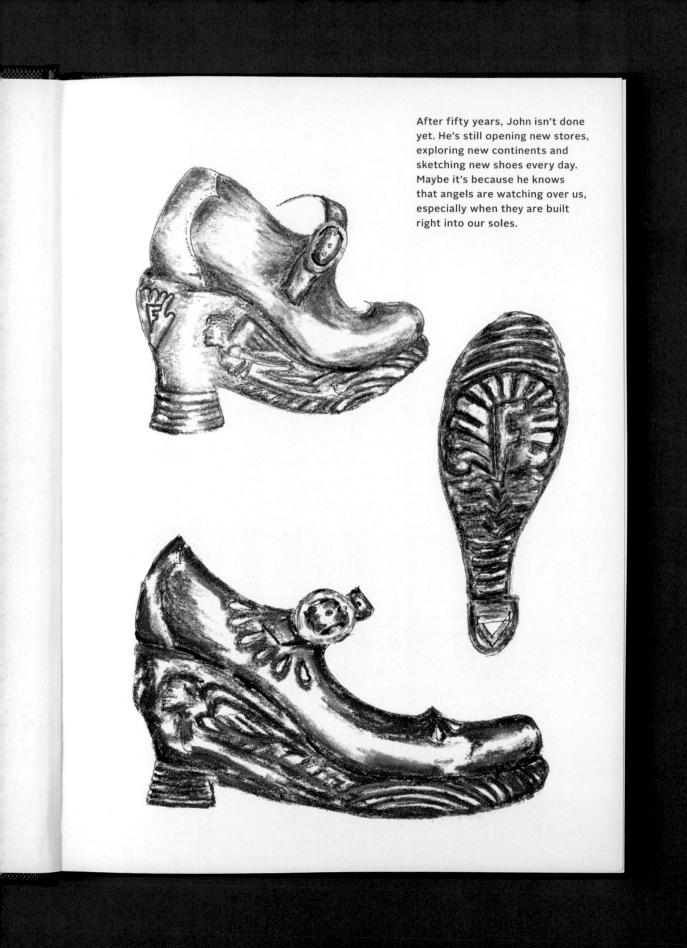

After fifty years, John isn't done yet. He's still opening new stores, exploring new continents and sketching new shoes every day. Maybe it's because he knows that angels are watching over us, especially when they are built right into our soles.

Know your mission,
do it well
and with style

**MYSTIC
TRAVELLER**
2020–

I DON'T LOOK BACK AND GO, I had a successful career. I go, I had a successful family. Our business is like a family, too. The Fluevogers and Fluevogologists are my family. Family is about love, and there has always been love in this family. As I'm nearing the end of my career, I have twenty-six stores, two-hundred-plus employees and a growing online presence. But my name has become my most important asset. As far as I know, there's hardly anyone left in the boutique business who is also designing stuff and remaining independent. That's a story in itself: How did John Fluevog do it?

Do you know how rare it is in the world of retail to be a sole owner? Not to have investors? Not to be at the whim of shareholders and directors and people in suits who have a say in what you do and how you do it? We could never have created the kind of designs we do if I didn't have the autonomy to make my own products the way I want. Aside from my father's initial $13,500, I've never had anyone put any money in the company. It's been a blessing. I haven't had to financially perform for somebody else. I can make mistakes and they're my mistakes.

What I didn't realize is that I was setting myself up for retail in a digital world. Being an outlier is hard if you own a single boutique. But online, having your own vibe and your own product and your own energy, it's an asset. I've been fortunate that I haven't lost control over my brand. They can't take my name away from me. I've maintained my integrity, but it hasn't been easy. Far from it.

Throughout my career, I've never really followed trends. I get influenced by things that are happening in the culture and I offer nods to them, but I'll always do a twist on the trend, not what everyone else is doing.

The most successful designs have been completely off the wall and had nothing to do with the fashion marketplace. They gave the company its identity. It's taken me a lifetime to build that identity.

I see what my mind wants me to see. I'll see things that have nothing to do with footwear. I see things in all sorts of places, when I travel to New York or London or Oaxaca, for instance. My design team calls me their "Mystic Traveller." It's true, I guess. I like telling stories that are part mystical and allude to something beyond the world that we live in. They make you dream and go to another place.

Most of the shoes you see are my own original designs. Sometimes they come to me in dreams, with celestial music and little fairy wings, so the design credit technically goes to God. So, here at John Fluevog Shoes, we officially have two designers: me and God. The design team thinks we sometimes argue over who's head designer, but you and I know what the answer is, right?

Of course, my designs haven't always clicked with everyone, and that includes the mainstream press. So often, the people who write for magazines and blogs are just looking for what's in and what's out, for the latest trend or the next trend. But my shoes don't follow trends. They just are. They're a little out of step with what's mainstream, and I'm OK with that. Some fashion writers also criticize the brand for not being one thing. I do high fashion and I do low fashion. I make unique shoes and unique people buy them. They can't put me in a box.

Now, of course, everything is changing because of the Internet and online retailing. Fashion is becoming less about one look, one trend. It's about individuality and

> **"Once upon a time Fox & Fluevog was a small start-up. John, young and incredibly handsome, Peter much older and not so handsome. Hey! If one had all the looks surely t'other must have had something, possibly the brains. You're wrong, my friend. The proof was in the separation. Just look at J's grand achievement."**
>
> PETER FOX, SHOE DESIGNER, FORMER PARTNER

self-expression. In that environment, me staying true to my own thing has become more accepted. You could say I was a step ahead. And the fashion press has taken notice.

In 2018, *Vogue* magazine published a story by Monica Kim on the thirtieth anniversary of the Munster, describing how it fits with current trends. "Now, everyone wants to be different," she wrote. "Couple that with real comfort? What could be better?" The same year, the *New York Times* published a fifteen-hundred-word Style section cover story by Linda Dyett, flatteringly entitled, "John Fluevog Is Cool Again. Maybe He Always Was." I was tickled to see her quoting experts saying they expect to see more of my designs in fashion media and among tastemakers "in today's trend-averse fashion universe." It'll be fun to see them catching up to our customers, who have always been like, "Your stuff resonates with me, it makes me feel so good."

But here's the thing. It's not just me or my shoes that are unique and special. So are you. You are the only person who's ever been made the way you are. People don't understand that the spirit inside them is unique. And I will go a step further and say they are loved. People don't have a good sense of who they are. If we can't express ourselves as individuals and celebrate that, society is so much poorer for it.

My life, my business, it hasn't always been easy. In fact, it's often been hard. I started out at a disadvantage because of my dyslexia. Well, I may be dyslexic, but I have a keen sense of what looks good. I came close to bankruptcy, twice. I almost died, twice. My heart was broken, twice. I experienced the agony of divorce and separation, but I also got to be father to three great kids, and now a grandfather five times over. I discovered that I am an artist, but I also have a logical side.

Now it's time to hand things over to someone else. I'm not retired—far from it!—but you know, I think I can let others take on some of the day to day. In fact, I've worked hard at creating a strategy that will ensure John Fluevog Shoes continues, no matter what. I've added more managers and executives (who are beloved members of the Fluevog community) to run the business, including my son Adrian, who is CEO. If anyone gets what the business is all about, it's someone who grew up with it. I've added more design staff, too. I still sketch every day and I still determine the vibe of the season, but I don't feel that I have to take a design through every step of the process. The idea is that even if I'm gone, Fluevog Shoes will be the same. That bothers me a little. I'm still fairly egotistical, I suppose; after all it is my name on the door. But then again, I don't plan to go anywhere anytime soon.

I'm still plugging away, still enjoying it. The company has been a vehicle for me to find out who I am and that my dyslexia and my weirdness is OK.

And I'm not done yet. There are causes that are close to my heart, that I want to support. I want to spend more time designing cars, and designing boats too, just having a good time. I consider myself successful and thankful.

"Many think of John Fluevog Shoes as kooky, eccentric, wild, fun. But to me, Fluevog— both the brand, including those who worked for the brand, and the man himself—was good and nice. And ethical. And human."

KIM HASTREITER, CO-FOUNDER AND
CO-EDITOR, *PAPER MAGAZINE*

We still plan to open more stores, but only if the right opportunity comes up. We're keen to involve people, certainly Fluevogers, in learning more about the operations of our brand. We've even begun having workshops where people can dye their own shoes. It's like back in the 1970s, when customers could customize their clogs.

It's a funny thing, for someone who's known for his colourful designs, but I never knew I was a creative person until I was in my thirties. I grew up in a religious household, but it wasn't a creative household. And now I know that really misses the point of who God is. We are all more artistic than we give ourselves credit for. We become vessels or conduits for spirituality, for faith, for the creative force. I could say I found God in myself—in my creativity and in my business. I just didn't know how to link the two for a very long time. It took even longer for me to realize that what I think is OK and that it has value.

In 1970, Peter Fox and I opened a boutique in Gastown, on Maple Tree Square, where the Angel clothing store is now. It changed the neighbourhood and it changed our lives. It changed a lot of lives. A decade later, I went out on my own; six years after that I started putting my name on my shoes. I didn't understand the meaning of that back then. But if I hadn't done it, I wouldn't be here right now, a global brand known for a bright, brave, colourfully unique style. And it's not just me—I could never have done it without the support, generosity and kindness of so many friends, family, staff, customers and, sometimes, perfect strangers who were there just at the right moment. I am grateful every day for every one of them, even if I sometimes forget to tell them. So, thank you.

There were successes and failures along the way. There were times when I stumbled, but God was there to help. I've been through heartbreak and near-bankruptcy, through illness and recovery, through crushing self-doubt and success beyond the wildest dreams of a dyslexic kid who had no idea what he wanted to be when he grew up.

So. All these years later. How did John Fluevog do it? It's really quite simple. He put his name on his shoes. JF

SECRET MESSAGE

John Fluevog has something to tell you.

Look at your sole to discover what it is.

On the bottom of most of my shoes, you will find a message. These messages are usually things that come to me while I'm drawing. Sometimes they're random and scattered. Sometimes they're very specific. These phrases form part of the energy and vibe around the shoes and are as important to me as the shoes themselves. The messages have a philosophical theme. A lot are about good and evil, justice, peace and inclusiveness. Things that are biblical at their core. I believe that we all can hear God. There's more to my messages than the words on your shoe. Here are some of the deeper meanings behind them.

PREVIOUS PAGE A shoe last with a message in front of the New Orleans store

A

ADRIAN

A thankful person is a happy person.

I first made this as a men's shoe and named it after my son Adrian. It eventually morphed into a women's shoe and became the foundation for many of the Fluevog shoes we have done over the years. Adrian has never been entirely happy about having a women's shoe named after him, but as it turns out, the slogan "A thankful person is a happy person" very much sums up his personality. Could it be that people become what we say they are?

ATV (ALL-TERRAIN VEHICLE)

Free your sole.

These shoes are all about being able to take us to more places than just the well-beaten path of life. We should all be free at a moment's notice to leave the road we are on and head off on a road that isn't so smooth. It may be harder, but taking the road less travelled can lead us to wonderful new experiences. We can veer off the freeway of life. We will be just fine—and probably more than fine. Be ready, be prepared. DDFT.

ANGEL

Resists alkali, water, acid, fatigue and Satan.

I designed the Angel soles out of a need to produce a more environmentally friendly sole that would eventually break down and not fill our Earth with toxins. Back then the fashion was to use footwear to ID oneself as a "hater," so I put angels into the sole and made them Satan resistant. Angels always resist Satan and hate is a stomping ground of Satan. This sole went on to be the company's best-selling product of the 1990s.

B

BAROQUE

There's no fashion like old fashion.

This shoe is part of my anti–fast fashion state of mind. We like to say, "Buy better, buy less." I love the idea that one wears something for years. I like to think of fashion as an expression of where we are on a continuum of time. We take things from the past and the future. I think time is not necessarily in a straight line. I believe these shoes could be brought out seventy-five years from now and be relevant. They are not a current short trend. They have their roots in our fashion DNA. One can walk in our history and our future in these shoes.

BALTHAZAR

A mystic traveller, following a star, bearing gifts from afar.

The name Balthazar—which means "one who protects the king"—is commonly attributed to one of the three Wise Men who followed the stars and studied ancient prophetic writings to bring gifts to the stable where Jesus was born. I liked the idea of following prophetic words. I also liked the idea of bringing gifts to the party! These messages might look odd and out of sync, but I believe that one day they will be considered forward-thinking. You could say I was following my own star.

BLIND FAITH

You need it to see where you are going.

Having blind faith to move forward when we don't see the future is a necessary part of life. Without a little faith we would be immobilized. It seems like the more risks we take the more we are rewarded. Even if the risks we take fail we are always better off to have tried than not. Step out and trust your sole.

BIG PRESENCE

Present yourself well.

Your uniqueness is your strength. These shoes are about being powerful because you are secure in who you are. You are bold because you like yourself. You are strong because you are 100 percent OK with who you are. You need no changes. No mistake was made. When you walk into a room you are OK with being noticed because you are OK with how you were made. Need to improve and grow? Sure, but don't change who you basically are. You stand out in a crowd and so you should. You are amazing and wondrous.

BEGIN

Let the dance begin.

Let life take you out for a dance. You move, it moves; life moves, you move. It's about working in community with the world around us, listening to the beat of the world and dancing with it. It's a dance of love.

Communicate with creation.

Our DNA is linked to the stars—we are part of the universe. The universe can communicate with us on deep sole levels. When I take time to listen, I can hear what creation is saying. Strange as it seems, I sometimes speak back and have conversations. This is how I came up with this heel. Ever wonder if what we see, touch and feel is all that there is? Ever wonder if other worlds are trying to communicate with us? What footwear would a celestial being wear? I have a feeling if they do wear shoes, they would wear these ones.

BELLEVUE

Keep pushing west and beyond your imagination.

Sometimes things just jump into my head. I was on the I-5 heading to Seattle from Vancouver, discussing this shoe with a design team member on the phone. When they asked what we should call it, I looked up and saw the Bellevue exit just before downtown Seattle. And that's how this shoe was named. The bigger picture: I had a vision given to me of an American Western town in the mid-1850s with all the various characters—the blacksmith, the cowboy, the hustlers, the saloon girls—and named these shoes after famous saloon girls. Following these visions has been a good idea for me.

CONQUER

Pick your battles!

Women are the ones behind the scenes organizing, planning and doing. When they hit the streets they need to look like and be the conquerors. Standing up for themselves and what is right, and pointing out what is wrong. I made these boots for street-battle warriors. "Look out, here I come," the person wearing these says. "We are all in a battle and we have won the right to conquer."

CHOICE

To love or to hate, the choice is yours.

During a phone conversation, the person I was talking to said they hated a mutual acquaintance. After hanging up I mused that there was no reason for this person to hate the other. It was a conscious choice to hate. The same way we choose to love someone, we choose to hate. So I wrote it down and sketched it out on a sole. It's our choice to love or to hate.

COSMOS

Created in the cosmos, worn on Earth.

Ever wonder where creative thoughts come from? How these visions come into your head? Have you ever soared in your mind to another place and seen things in a new way? The creative process is often like that. Going to another place can come in different ways at different times and different ways for each of us. I sense the creative comes from outside of me. I'm only a receptacle. I need to have my antennae up to hear. I seem out of tune a lot of times, but once in a while I see wonderful things that I draw or write down and in those times I feel joyful. I know the things I see are pure and right for me. They are truly gifts. When I did this shoe, with its clear sole, I felt the joy.

EARL OF WARWICK

Let down the drawbridge, Earl! It's time to party!

Family folklore has it that the English Earl of Warwick went adventuring along the coast of Norway, where he met my great-grandmother, and they had a child: my grandmother. I have never wanted to investigate this story as I like the the mystery of it. I have visited the earl's castle (very nice, thanks) and wondered if I could have a small right to stay a night or two? Barring that, I drew this shoe and named the family after him.

EXECUTOR

Execute your will.

I designed these shoes for the executive in all of us. We all are executives in our own way. We decide what we are going to do and we go about executing it. We see something, we put the pieces together, get others on board and make it happen. Before we do all that we have to know what we want. Know what you want and why, and then go out and make it happen.

ENTRANCE

Make a fitting entrance. Stand in the liberty.

Make a fitting entrance. When you walk into a room be bold, be strong and walk straight in. Know where you are going, don't be faint of heart. You are in control. Don't let others take who you are from you. My hope is that when you wear these shoes they will encourage you to be bold and stand up for your rights. You are amazing—be strong and be powerful because you are.

ENNEAGRAM

Be your true self.

A Jesuit priest named Richard Robe introduced me to the Enneagram. It's an ancient personality test, dating from before the time of Christ and probably coming from the Sufis or the mystic wise men, who had all but disappeared. The test proved amazingly accurate for my personality. It is a further explanation on how to understand and get along with the different personality types in our world and why certain people have "go-to reactions." I wanted to highlight the history and insight of this method of personality testing. It was all done over two thousand years ago—amazing!

ESOTERIC TEMPTATIONS

Temptations...be vigilant, protect your sole.

These shoes were born in the 1980s, a combination of parts and pieces of shoes I did back in the day. They have withstood the test of time. The name started in the East End of London where the first ones were made. The East End girls could not say "Fluevog" so it came out "frugal" and that then became the name in the late '80s. I renamed the family in 2017 when we redesigned it and called it "Esoteric Temptations." I was thinking of all the temptations that we encounter in life and how some of them are so utterly damaging to us. The word *esoteric* meant to me "otherworldly" and I have a feeling that some temptations do come from another world and have an exotic appeal. I have always imagined heavenly beings wearing these shoes with pleasure.

FAIRWAY

Reckless chances, emotional thrills, sensory delights.

I named these shoes after the excitement of the circus fairway. Walking the fairways with the sights, smells, colours and sounds is like no other place on Earth. It transports us to a make-believe place. Wavy and skewed, the shoes take us to another world of fun and sensual pleasure. For me the Fairway is about the party of life. The otherworldly feeling one gets at the fairway at an amusement park. That off-kilter party feeling.

F

FUTURE ANGEL

Your sole will direct your future.

Angel soles have been a part of Fluevog history for years. I introduced the Future Angels as a reminder that if we want to know what our future will look like, we should take a close look at what we are doing today. Strange but true, it's not a mystery to see what's in our future. We are doing it today.

I

ISHSHOES

Iron out your Ishshoes.

We all have them and it's up to us to fix them. No one else can do it for us. A friend who is a marriage and family counsellor once said to me, "Ishshoes would be a good name for a shoe. If you don't deal with your issues someone else will and when they do, it will hurt a lot more." The point is we have the power and obligation to take hold of our issues and conquer them.

LISTEN UP

Girls like to be heard.

Well, we all do, but sometimes girls talk and boys aren't listening. When I did these shoes I had the thought that these shoes command attention in all ways. They're about respect and strength. With these shoes on, a woman has the power and men have to "listen up."

K

KITSCHY KITSCHY BOOM BOOM

F is for all things that give hope.

This name popped into my mind when I made these shoes. I envisioned the girl who would wear these walking down the street with an air of authority, looking like and knowing she was all that and a piece of cake! Larger than life moving with grace and poise. In her own world and knowing she looks fabulous, she moves with purpose and is happy with who she is. Boom boom boom.

L

LA

Rise above earthly restraints.

I was in Los Angeles, and it seemed to me everyone there was just following quick trends and not really understanding themselves and why they did things. They all seemed to be desperately trying to fit in. So I designed these boots and wrote this poem: Always hold on to the truth. Don't let others sway your heart. Don't compromise yourself for the sake of temporal grooviness. Be separate from the crowd that's awash with normality by standing on a firm foundation. Never waver in your faith and above all, please wear my shoes.

157

M

MELLOW

Go wear the spirit flows.

These flowing lines are the expression of how I flow through life. Sometimes the stream of life flows easy and shows you truths. Other times, you're swimming upstream, trying to do your own thing and it does not work so well. We may as well have angels and the sole to help guide us along the way. These shoes flow. Relax and let the stream of the spirit take you. Be immersed in the flow of the universe; knowing that you can trust and not fear is the best place to be. I'm learning how to trust and not fear, to go with the stream and not against it.

MEMORIES

My memories of love are of you.

I did these shoes when I was in a dark place, feeling the loss of love from a certain person. (Life is not all sunshine.) I got through it, thank the Lord, and now the memory has faded and I'm left with the shoe I did, and I still like the shoe! So that's a good thing. Maybe love never goes away—it just morphs into something else.

MISSION

Know your mission, do it well and with style.

I believe we all have a mission in our lives. I know I do. Mine is to move people from one place to another in style. To hopefully take them to a little higher place. Whether it's make-believe or real. My job is to make people feel special. We all need to feel special and I hope my shoes do that. While I was designing these shoes, a special friend of mine who had given me loads of encouragement passed away. I decided to name this style of the Mission family "Wendy" after her. Wendy was a person who knew highs and lows, but overall knew her mission and accomplished it with great style.

MIRACLES

Miracles are the surprises of the soul.

Meeting that special person who influences our life can be a miracle. Believe it or not, getting dress shoes to fit well is a bit of a miracle, too. These shoes fit very well, thanks to my friend and ex-partner Peter Fox, who shared his best-fitting lasts with me. So in honour of him, I named these shoes Miracles.

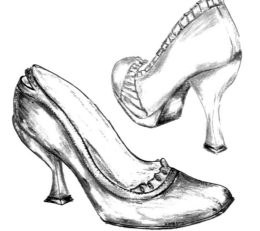

ON COURSE

Stay the course.

Stay sharp, stay in the lines, don't vary your course. This practice has served me well in the business of making shoes. Keeping within the boundaries of the straight lines. Not going off course on a different program when things get a little hard. Set the boundaries and stay the course. To me these shoes have always had a nautical feel with all their straight lines. When sailing close to shore, it's always good to set a point and sail toward it.

Your love makes me sing.

"Arise, my darling, my beautiful one, come with me." This saying is an excerpt from the Song of Solomon in the Old Testament of the Bible. It's seen as an allegory for all of love. When we're in love we understand beauty and see the beauty in all things. I like the romance of poetry and song. The thought of someone breaking into song to express their innermost feelings is so old-fashioned, but touches and delights if it's ever done. I wanted to touch the people who wore these shoes and to let them know they are loved and part of the greater operetta of life, the operetta of Fluevog.

PREPARE

Prepare for the future, choose well today.

I was thinking of global warming when I designed the Prepares. I was considering footwear that was needed in the future. Shoes that would keep one out of high floodwaters while looking good. It had to be a distinctive Fluevog shoe with treads on the sole for traction. Good height so you can see where you are going, all with style, and thus the Prepare was born and named. Life throws some strange curves at us from time to time: make sure you're prepared.

POSER

Yes, you are. You're super cute. I said so.

I like the idea of posing. Sometimes in life there is a place for posing. It's the idea that you can be striking against any background and in any place. It's the concept that you are saying, "Hey, I like myself." Having sold a lot of women's shoes over the years, I've always enjoyed watching women look at themselves in a mirror and strike a pose as they're deciding what shoes to buy or not. When the stars align and the feeling is right and someone says, "Hey, you look cute in those," it's bing bam boom and they walk out of the shop with shoes that say, "I look cute in these." There's nothing like a nice super cute shoe to strike a pose in, and this is it. I said so.

PROVOGS

Oh that my weary feet could soar to places never seen before and float on dreaming wings of grace above this dour and earthly place.

I was in a mood at the time I made this sole. The poem I wrote (seen in the message above) expressed my feelings at that moment. And from time to time I still feel that way.

159

Tough love sucks.

Sometimes under extreme circumstances we need someone close to us to administer tough love. What happens is we go down a path that others can see has a bad ending, but we ourselves ignore the sign posts. Someone needs to come along and say, "If you don't stop this, I'll stop being your friend," or something drastic like that. This is such a bad idea for someone else to have to do this and for the person hearing it to have to deal with it. So I say, "Tough love sucks all around. Best to just not need it."

QUEEN OF PRUSSIA

Guard your boundaries.

This is one of the Queen family of shoes, which I designed as a tribute to those who seek truth and wisdom to unlock the secrets of the universe and earn their crown. Prussia, along with its queen, disappeared from the map as we know it because she failed to protect her borders. On the back of the heel, I inscribed the secret symbols of the Fluevog language—each symbol represents a phrase that you can mix and match for your own secret message. I named these shoes for the need we all have to guard our hearts and boundaries, or like the country Prussia your identity will disappear and be forgotten. Be strong, stand up and respect yourself.

QUEEN OF THE SKIES

Be the queen of the skies.

Seek infinite, everlasting beauty. A true queen has lasting beauty and influence. Not trendy, she instead looks for lasting style. I could imagine celestial beings wearing these shoes through eternity. True fashion fit for an everlasting queen.

QUEEN TRANSCENDENT

Exceed your own expectations.

Transcend your earthly boundaries. Move from your drudgery of day to day, and jump into the stream of love and let it carry you. Don't try and hang onto the branches that lie on the side of the stream. Enjoy the flow of the spirit. Let go of things that bind you, and have faith that the stream will take you to wonderful new places you never dreamed of.

TRUTH

Truth and integrity since 1970.

These are the evolution of the Pilgrim, one of the first shoes I designed, back in 1986. I was influenced by a girl I saw on a Vancouver street, wearing cowboy boots that were too big for her so the toes curled up in the air. I carved up a shoe last and had my shoemaker friend Ken Rice make the first pair, complete with a buckle from a dress store down the street. And so the Pilgrim shoe was born. Now renamed Truth, it has been a constant in the Fluevog shoe range for nearly thirty-five years and shows no sign of stopping.

WEAREVER

Wearever you go, give thanks.

Giving thanks is a theme in my life as it's not my go-to emotion. I have to work at being thankful. When I drew this sole and its family it was really a reminder to myself and, hopefully, the wearer to give thanks in all things. I wanted a pretty shoe that also wore well. Hence the Wearever and a reminder to myself that when I do give thanks, even when things don't seem good, it changes me into a happier, more positive person. Now if only I could remember to do it more often.

VOG TOGETHER

The more we Vog together, the happier we will be.

I like the idea of community. The idea that we are all of one mind and sole. We work together in community with each of us playing a part to make the whole better. Fluevogers are an eclectic group. They are made up of people from all walks of life and interests, but I have found they are all of one mind when it comes to some things. They all have a love of individual expression and are not afraid to express it. They are not afraid to wear footwear that stands out and sets them apart. They all like going to another place in time and space: Vogville.

VIEWS

Things look different from a distance.

I like the idea of being able to see above the crowd with high heels, figuratively and in reality. When I look above the crowd, I can see the future much clearer. Looking above and ahead helps us live our lives with a greater sense of purpose.

INDEX

ACKNOWLEDGEMENTS

WHEN I BEGAN MY CAREER fifty years ago, I could never have imagined making it past the first year let alone writing a book, so I'm as tickled as can be that you're holding this one in your hands. But just like creating a shoe takes a team of dedicated people, so does making a book as unique as this one. So to each and every person who poured their heart and sometimes nervous sweat into this project, I owe my thanks.

First and foremost, thank you to my team at John Fluevog Shoes, who did heroic work in researching the photos, stories and bits of information accumulated over fifty admittedly disorganized and sometimes chaotic years. Leading that team is my chief marketing officer Stephen Bailey, whose title doesn't really reflect all he does. He captures the very essence of what Fluevog is all about and this book would not have been possible without him.

Thank you, too, to our team of incredibly talented people at Fluevog HQ. This book would not be what it is if not for the efforts of Kristin Liu, Alison Tan, Luiza Libardi and countless others who supported us with their unmatched expertise.

Thank you to the team at LifeTree Media, to publisher Maggie Langrick, who believed so strongly in my story, as well as project editor Joanne Sasvari, art director Natalie Olsen, editorial director Sarah Brohman and publishing coordinator Jesmine Cham. Thank you all for telling my story so beautifully.

I must also thank my friend Peter Fox and a community of others who kindly walked down memory lane with me as we worked to piece together my past.

My most sincere gratitude also goes to my family. To my parents, who I miss every day, to my wife, Ruth, who was always ready to catch my mistakes before I made them, to my son Adrian, who made sure the business was running smoothly while I was dreaming about the past, and to Britta, Jonathan and my grandchildren, who keep me grounded and mindful of what a lucky man I am to have them.

And finally, thank you to Fluevogers worldwide for spreading the word, celebrating weirdness and helping me stay in business this whole time—I hope you have enjoyed the journey so far. To each one of you: **you are all more creative than you think you are.**

Copyright © 2019 by John Fluevog

19 20 21 22 23   5 4 3 2 1

All rights reserved. No part of this book may be reproduced, stored in a retrieval system or transmitted, in any form or by any means, without the prior written consent of the publisher or a license from The Canadian Copyright Licensing Agency (Access Copyright). For a copyright license, visit www.accesscopyright.ca or call toll free to 1-800-893-5777.

Cataloguing data available from Library and Archives Canada

ISBN: 978-1-928055-53-2 (trade edition)
ISBN: 978-1-928055-70-9 (Fluevog special edition — blue)
ISBN: 978-1-928055-62-4 (Fluevog special edition — gold)
ISBN: 978-1-928055-68-6 (Fluevog special edition — white)
ISBN: 978-1-928055-69-3 (Fluevog special edition — black)
ISBN: 978-1-928055-54-9 (EPUB)

Project editor: Joanne Sasvari
Book design and art direction: Natalie Olsen
Author portrait: Andy Dixon

Published by LifeTree Media Ltd.
www.lifetreemedia.com

Distributed in Canada by Greystone Books Ltd.
www.greystonebooks.com

Distributed in the U.S. by Publishers Group West

Printed and bound in Singapore

Every effort has been made to ascertain ownership and copyright in the use of images. In the event of an inadvertent omission or error, please notify the publisher.

Grateful acknowledgement is made to the following sources for permission to reprint images from previously published material.

Portraits of John Fluevog on pages 1 and 168 by Andy Dixon

Photograph of Toronto Queen Street store on page 4 by Ryan Tacay

Photograph of Jaguar Mark X on page 28 © Keystone Press / Alamy Stock Photo

McCabe & Mrs. Miller movie poster on page 49 © TCD/Prod.DB/ Alamy Stock Photo

Shoe catalogues on pages 70–71, 73, 75–77, 79–85, 88–89 by Dave Webber

Photograph of Lady Miss Kier on page 92 by Simon Fowler

Photograph of Madonna on page 93 by Mark Reinstein, courtesy of Getty Images

Photograph of Absolut Vodka shoes on page 95, courtesy of Bata Shoe Museum

Photograph of Robin Williams on page 97 by Mary Ellen Mark

Photograph of Jack White on page 112 by David James Swanson

Photograph of Lady Miss Kier on page 115 by Michael Halsband

Photograph of Sasha Velour's shoes on page 124 by Mettie Ostrowski, courtesy of Witch House PR

Photograph of Sasha Velour on page 124 by Tanner Abel, courtesy of Witch House PR

Photograph of Lady Gaga on page 133 © MediaPunch Inc / Alamy Stock Photo

Photograph of sketchbook on pages 22, 46, 62, 90, 106, 128, 144 © BONNINSTUDIO/Shutterstock.com

Resists alkali, water, acid, fatigue and Satan.

John Fluevog is a celebrated Canadian shoe designer known for his witty and unconventional style. Colourful, Art Deco–inspired and inscribed with uplifting messages, his shoes are among the most distinctive footwear of the last fifty years. They have graced dance floors and boardrooms alike and are worn by everyone from Alice Cooper to Lady Gaga to nurses, teachers, lawyers, bikers, baristas and someone down your street. Today, John Fluevog owns 27 stores across North America, Europe and Australia. He lives in Vancouver, still sketches new designs every day and knows he's weird.